This book may be returned to any Wiltshire
library. To renew this book phone your library
or visit the website: www.wiltshire.gov.uk

Wiltshire Council
Where everybody matters

NICHOLAS BREALEY
PUBLISHING

London • Boston

First published in the UK by
Nicholas Brealey Publishing in 2012

3–5 Spafield Street
Clerkenwell, London
EC1R 4QB
Tel: +44 (0)20 7239 0360
Fax: +44 (0)20 7239 0370

20 Park Plaza, Suite 1115A
Boston
MA 02110, USA
Tel: 888 BREALEY
Fax: (617) 523 3708

www.nicholasbrealey.com
www.peterallison.com

ISBN 978-1-85788-566-8
eISBN 978-1-85788-985-7

Map and illustrations by Guy Holt

British Library Cataloguing in Publication Data
A catalogue record for this book is available from the British Library.

FSC
Mixed Sources

Printed in the UK by Clays Ltd, St Ives plc

While escaping a desk, hitting the road and collecting new experiences is fun to do, there are always treasured people you leave behind. In my case these are my wonderful sister Laurie—the only person I've known my whole life—and her two children, Riley and Molly, plus my oldest friends, Nick Goodwin (has it really been a quarter of a century?), Hayden Jones and Marc Butler. I love you all, despite the names I call you.

Contents

Cartagena

VENEZUELA

GUYANA

FRENCH
GUIANA

Bogotá

SURINAME

COLOMBIA

The Andes

Quito
Napo River
Coca

SACHA LODGE
Yasuni
National
Park

ECUADOR

The Amazon

The Andes

BRAZIL

Lima

PERU

The
Pantanal

Lake
Titicaca

La Paz
Cochabamba

Coroico
Villa Tunari
Santa Cruz de la Sierra

Brasilia

Salar de Uyuni

BOLIVIA

Uyuni

Lago Colorado

San Pedro de Atacama

PARAGUAY

Rio de Janeiro

The Andes

CHILE

ARGENTINA

Pacific

Ocean

URUGUAY

Santiago

Buenos Aires

Chillán
Concepción

Linares

Patagonia

Puerto Montt
Bariloche

Atlantic

Ocean

The Andes

Patagonia

El Chaltén
El Calafate

Tierra
del Fuego

Ushuaia

0   500 KM

N
W   E
S

Introduction: Slapped on the Streets of Cebu

It's all the labradors' fault. I grew up with two of them, as well as a brave cat who brutalised the dogs, an outdoor goldfish pond regularly raided by a red-bellied black snake, and the odd sheep—our neighbour had one because it made the perfect lazy man's lawnmower. My single mother frequently borrowed Bunty for the same lawn-trimming purpose, though the poor creature was often distracted from its hungry work by the attention lavished on it by my sister and me. In our otherwise normal Sydney suburb this animal seemed to us quite exotic.

But it was always the dogs I loved best, with their unswerving devotion and affection, and their endearing habit of accompanying me everywhere I went on my bicycle. My closeness to them taught me to pay attention to all the animals around me, not just those with a collar. Showing early signs of the wildlife nut I would become, I wanted a relationship with the possums and frogmouths in the yard at night as well as my dogs.

Then, when I was sixteen, I went to Japan for a year. During that time a series of near-biblical plagues overtook our city of Okayama, a couple of hours north-east of Hiroshima. First came praying mantises, which begat a plague of frogs that emerged en masse from the city's open drains in pursuit of the bounty of insects. Close behind them came the snakes. For the town this was a nightmare, but I was delighted. My host family's cat was the only one to share my enthusiasm; she caught the snakes alive and dumped them proudly at the bare feet of whichever startled family member was at home. 'Piitaa!' would come the cry, and I would sally from my room, scoop up the snake and take it back outside. 'Sayonara,' I would farewell each snake. 'Hiss,' the snake would reply, if at all.

I always wanted to be around wild animals, but saw no practical way to do it. The path to law school that was expected of me by my parents was as personally appealing as the snakes had been to the residents of Okayama, so when I returned to Australia I dropped out of high school. I worked for a harbour cruise company for two years, then decided to travel for at least a year, to somewhere that had an abundance of wildlife. Maybe then I would go to law school.

I had two places in mind, both inspired by the nature documentaries I loved on television. Either Africa or South America would allow me to spend the time that I craved with animals. So in late 1993, a few days before my nineteenth birthday, I used the most rigorous and scientific method I could think of to decide between these destinations, and tossed a coin.

Africa came up heads that day, and the coin-flip changed my life. Within two weeks I was on a plane to Zimbabwe. I thought I would stay in Africa for a year, but my passion for wildlife shone through while I was visiting a safari camp, and I was offered a job behind the bar. Over the next seven years I worked my way up and became a safari guide, a camp manager, and ultimately a teacher of guides for one of the largest safari companies on the continent. In that time I had some of the best experiences with animals that anyone could wish for. I witnessed an elephant giving birth, was charged by lions, had a leopard walk into my tent, and made friends with a family of cheetahs who would allow me to lie down beside them. In fact I had enough experiences that I was able to write two books about them.

Somehow through all of this I retained the nagging doubt that I was cheating at life and that at some point I would need to get a real job. The sort that grown-ups had.

'You're a fool,' one of my colleagues told me when I said I was leaving to head back to the real world of nine to five.

'You're good at this,' some of the kinder ones said.

But it was time to be a normal adult.

I have no idea why I thought I'd be good at that.

•

On my return to Sydney from Africa in late 2001 I felt too old for law school and applied for an array of different jobs instead, fielding interview questions such as: 'And what skills do you think you can bring us?' In truth I felt I had little to offer the mainstream office world. 'Um, I can stare down a charging elephant,' I'd joke on occasion. After a somewhat startled pause the inevitable response to this would be along the lines of, 'Interesting, yes, but not something we value here at McDonald's.'

After enduring countless rejections and dropping several rungs on the ladder of self-respect, I eventually got a job—which turned into a series of jobs—that at least paid the rent.

I also fell in love and felt certain enough about the relationship to get engaged. In the next few years we accumulated the things adults do, mainly furniture and debt. For the first time I owned more than I could carry on my back, and even if I didn't like the sensation, I believed I was doing what I was supposed to.

I was on a work trip to the Philippines six years after meeting my fiancée when I realised that the life we had together didn't feel right to me. One day I was walking down the street in Cebu and was hit with a sudden shot of wary adrenalin, as though if I wasn't alert there could be trouble. It was invigorating. It felt like being back in Africa. It felt like being slapped awake from a long sleepwalk. It felt like coming home. Only then did I realise that I'd been turning grey from the inside out, and had become the cliché of the dissatisfied worker bee. I'd spent most of the last seven years waiting for five o'clock, hanging out for Friday, going on holiday only to stress out because I couldn't relax fast enough. Perhaps some adults aren't meant to be in one place. It is like being left-handed: no matter how good you become at using your right hand, your nature still insists you are something else. Nomads are the same.

While some people allow the hollowness of their lives to consume them until they are at zero, so blank they merely exist, others rebel. Some men find solace in sports. Some have affairs. Others dress as a woman and insist on being addressed as Gertrude. My way of breaking the shackles is to go looking for animals. As a teenager I had travelled to escape my life; now I wanted to do it to have one. 'I think you're being a fool,' my fiancée said with more sadness than harshness when I told her I wanted to travel open-endedly again, with her this time, working part-time as a safari guide. 'We've built a life here!' She indicated the apartment we lived in, and our possessions within it.

'I want experiences,' I answered softly, 'not stuff.'

'Stuff? This isn't stuff! It's security!'

But what felt like security to her felt like a prison to me. She wouldn't come with me and I couldn't stay. It was the hardest decision of my life, but we broke up and, taking little more than some clothes, I left.

Over the years I had often wondered what would have happened if the coin that sent me to Africa had landed tails-up that day. So in late 2009, sixteen years later and hopefully an equivalent number of years wiser, I made my way to Santiago, Chile, ready to seek out the continent's best, weirdest and maddest wilderness experiences. This time around, though, I was no longer a teenager and was wary of further injuring my weakened knees and sorely abused back (almost ten years' driving off road has compressed my spine; I'm sure I'm an inch shorter than I was before). But the continent holds challenges—dense rainforests, high mountains, waterless deserts, vast and lonely steppes, as well as dangerous animals like jaguars, pumas and bushmaster snakes—that I wanted to seek out.

Whereas Africa always appears brown in documentaries, every nature show I'd ever watched about South America has been in glorious technicolour. Evolution seems to have taken some strange, strong medicine before setting to work there, producing improbable, extraordinary creatures. In Africa I could be trampled by elephants or consumed by lions; the most dangerous animal in South America is a kaleidoscopic frog so toxic that just touching it can be lethal. There is a bird called the hoatzin which has evolved my favourite strategy for evading the attention of predators, a solution so simple that anything else seems a waste of energy—it is too smelly to eat. Then there are sloths, whose legendary slowness actually works for them, making them hard to pick out among the foliage in which they live—this, along with a groove in each of their hairs in which camouflaging algae grows, makes them almost invisible. I wanted to see all these animals and more; but above all, more than any bird, fish or reptile, I wanted to fulfil an ambition born of all those nature documentaries I'd watched as a child: to see a wild jaguar.

But my plans are usually only good for one thing—laughing at in hindsight—so, armed with bad Spanish, coupled with dangerous levels of curiosity and a record of poor judgement, I set off to tackle whatever South America could throw at me.

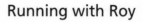

'See a jaguar? Mwah ha ha! You're more likely to fall pregnant to a llama,' said my friend Marguerite Gomez as we drove from Santiago airport to her home.

Marguerite's husband, Harris, gave me an apologetic look at his wife's bluntness, but as she and I were old friends from Africa days I was far from offended. And I also knew she was right. Jaguars live in the jungle, a hard place to see anything that isn't right in front of you, given the usually impenetrable foliage. Adding to the challenge, the jaguar is the master of stealth. If they don't want to be seen, chances are they won't be.

But if it was going to be easy, why would I bother?

'I'm going to see one, along with everything else natural that I can,' I countered.

'Sure,' said Marguerite, as you would to someone who's just told you they have access to Nigeria's hidden billions.

The birds of South America were another draw for me, as during my safari career I had picked up the hobby of birdwatching, a habit which to some people is as sexy as flatulence (at best when I admit to it I get a restrained smile that clearly indicates the listener wants to hear no more).

I stayed for a week with Marguerite, Harris and their two young daughters. Harris shared with me the delight of staggeringly good

Chilean wines while Marguerite mixed the best pisco sour on the continent. (The pisco sour is a wonderful cocktail that both Chile and Peru claim to have invented; at times this argument becomes so heated you wouldn't be surprised if it led to military action—not as improbable as it sounds considering the countries once waged war over bird poo.)

When I arrived in Santiago I hadn't expected to see many animals around the city of high rises and office blocks, but on only my second day Marguerite summoned me upstairs, insisting I bring binoculars with me. Through them I saw an enormous bird soaring over the not-so-distant, snow-frosted peaks of the Andes.

'Condor?' Marguerite asked, grinning, knowing how much I would enjoy it if it was.

'Wow,' was my eloquent reply. That was all it could be; there was nothing else so huge in the skies that wasn't man-made.

The condor was the bird I'd most wanted to see. The sighting was a great welcome to South America and more than I could have asked for—until I hit somewhere more wild I would have been content with the mockingbirds and hummingbirds that visited the Gomezes' garden.

Santiago is a city occasionally reviled by travellers seeking the famed chaos and liveliness of South America, but I think this is unfair. While it may lack the exuberance of Buenos Aires and the sexiness of Rio, it has its charms, such as the fancy, brightly coloured buildings jammed beside cheap student bars with plastic chairs and umbrellas advertising beer, sharing a bonhomie until late into every night. Food is excellent in the city, and levels of service high. In short it was the perfect introduction to South America. While I was impressed with Santiago's orderliness and cleanliness, I was now to set off for Bolivia, a place that Harris said was so undeveloped not even Chileans visited.

'Good,' I replied cockily, to hide my own doubts about the decision I'd made in leaving Sydney. Was a nomadic life really feasible? Was I too old for this? Was I, perhaps, now too wise to have the sort of adventures that Africa had given me?

In a life peppered with moments of grand idiocy, the last thought was the most foolish so far.

●

In central Bolivia, in a patch of forest near the small town of Villa Tunari, lives a puma. His russet fur shows that he is a jungle puma (mountain pumas have grey coats), but he wasn't born there. At the age of around six weeks he was confiscated by wildlife authorities from a marketplace. The wildlife authorities then delivered him to a group called Inti Wara Yassi who take in such animals, care for them as best they can and then release them if possible. This particular puma has noble features, is strongly muscled, and deserves a mighty name. But he is called Roy. And I was tied to him for a month.

I got to know Roy while I was volunteering at Parque Machia, a small reserve where hundreds of animals live and the first stop on my quest to learn about South America's wilderness. After a flight from Santiago to crumbly old Santa Cruz de la Sierra, one of Bolivia's larger towns, I'd hopped onto a surprisingly modern bus. Its passengers were mainly locals, with a smattering of backpackers. Among the locals were bowler hat- and poncho-wearing women, a sight that went from captivating to commonplace as we passed through a bewildering series of villages. After a day of travelling I stumbled from the bus halfway between Santa Cruz and Cochabamba into the town of Villa Tunari.

The local mayor runs a small tourist attraction next to the Parque Machia reserve, where visitors—mainly Bolivians—come to see monkeys who are unusually relaxed around humans. The reserve also has bears, ocelots, coatis, macaws, eagles and pumas, but the tourists don't get to see these unless they meet one as it crosses the trails with its handlers. For the animals' wellbeing most of them see no one but their handlers.

While Bolivians founded and manage Parque Machia, most of the staff is made up of short-term volunteers from every corner of the globe. The group of volunteers while I was at Inti consisted of a close-knit cluster of Israelis, a handful of French, a few Americans, a disproportionately large number of Australians, one or two Italians and a lone Norwegian. (He was quite thrilled when two Danes arrived, since he could understand them.) We pieced together communication through intersecting languages, and the shared love of animals that had drawn us to this punishment.

Within hours of arriving at Parque Machia, I joined eight other new volunteers to listen to an Australian called Bondy give us a rundown on the park. This was to be our induction, we would learn what animals we would be working with during our time there. We had very different backgrounds and reasons for being there, but we were all excited about the work ahead. 'My sort of people,' I thought, and was pleased with my decision to come here, even though ensconced volunteers had already warned me that most days were filled with grimy work. 'A monkey just spunked on me!' one woman exclaimed moments after I introduced myself at a communal table. 'That's after already being shat and pissed on this week!' (It probably says a lot about me that I still found her quite attractive.)

What had drawn me to this place, and presumably the others too, was the philosophy of Inti Wara Yassi (which means 'Sun, Earth, Moon' in three local languages). Its founders and managers believe that no animal deserves to live its life in a cage, and so every single creature in its care has time in the jungle each day. Monkeys being vile was surely as bad as it could get, right? At the induction, Bondy talked to us about the different animals in the reserve: the monkeys and macaws, as well as less familiar creatures like tayra and coatis, and finally the cats.

'You have to be fit to be a Roy Boy—that's what we call the volunteers who work with Roy,' said Bondy. 'He covers a lot of ground each session, most of it at a run, over rough terrain that can snap an ankle or smash your knees. He nails the guys with him all the time so they have to stay on their toes. And when I say "nail" I mean that he grabs the back of your legs with his paws then bites you on the knee. So you have to be fit—fit and a little bit crazy.'

'That,' I thought, 'sounds wildly irresponsible, dangerous, and maybe a bit stupid.' 'That,' I said, raising my hand, 'sounds like me.'

'He gets a bit more unpredictable when there are new guys,' Roy Boy Mick warned me the morning after the briefing, as I stumbled along behind him on the steep trail up to Roy's enclosure, already feeling a burn in my thigh muscles.

Yet another Australian, Mick had been at Parque Machia for three months, well beyond the average length of stay for a volunteer. (Mick was an example to me of a theory I have that Australians often stay in places a long time in dread of the flight home.) He had already spent four weeks of his three months with Roy, and despite frequent abuse at the paws and teeth of the puma (if a bun had been placed on either side of his knee it would have made a convincing hamburger) he was clearly in love with the big cat. With us was Adrian, the Norwegian, who had been training to work with Roy only a few days.

'What do you mean by "unpredictable"?' I asked.

'Well, usually he'll only run in certain places, downhill mainly, and he runs after he takes a dump,' explained Mick. 'But when there's a new guy he might drag us around all morning. He also gets jumpier.'

'Jumpy, like nervous?'

'Nah, mate—jumpy like he jumps on you and bites your knee. It'll happen to you, don't worry.'

Don't worry? The idea of a puma jumping on me seemed a perfectly reasonable thing to be concerned about.

Roy wasn't a huge animal, about the size of a German shepherd, but beneath his red fur he was much more heavily muscled than any dog. His fur was smooth and horse-like in texture, and he had patches of an impossibly brilliant white around the nose and mouth, counterpointed by eye markings of deep ebony. His facial features were surprisingly delicate; most male cats have squared-off muzzles and a certain tightness around the eyes, but Roy had the softer, smoother features of a female.

It was a thrill to touch Roy the first time, and remained so every time after that. This was a puma! I watched Mick clip a ten-metre rope around his waist with a sturdy carabiner, before connecting the other end of the rope to Roy's collar.

'He usually runs a bit up this first slope,' Mick warned over his shoulder, his eyes sticking resolutely to Roy's muscular shoulders.

'How far he runs gives you an idea what sort of morning you'll have,' added Adrian.

Known in the park as the 'Nordic Giant', Adrian had recently completed two years' military service in the Norwegian army, and was used to marching, but he laughed at me when I suggested that his military service had probably prepared him for the trails we were about to use.

'No way,' he said. 'The army had nothing like this.'

That morning Mick took the lead and Adrian was in the position called, without derogatory intent, 'number two'. I was told that I had one task only—to keep up.

As soon as we set off Roy ran up the slope from his enclosure, but instead of pausing at the top he kept on running, racing through narrow gaps in jauntily flowered bushes with grabby thorns, then dashing along a creek bed over slimy mossy rocks before sprinting up yet another muddy bank, while I grasped at branches and ferns, trying to stay close behind them. After running for what felt like a very long time, I wanted to ask how normal this pace was and how long Roy could be expected to keep it up. Unfortunately, someone had let a swarm of scorpions loose in my lungs and I couldn't speak, so I just grimly sprinted on, wondering if it would be considered rude to vomit.

By the end of the morning session I noticed Mick and Adrian shooting surreptitious glances at each other and began to suspect that Roy's behaviour was even more extreme than what he usually put a new wrangler through. They probably didn't want me to know this, and were seeing if I could tough it out.

At lunchtime, Adrian waited with Roy, who had the run of an exercise area during our break, while Mick and I staggered back to the main area. We sat side by side and ate a disappointingly vegetarian meal (my body was demanding protein after such abuse), no one else apparently wanting to sit next to such conspicuously perspiring men. I had come to Parque Machia hoping to do some good and have some fun at the same time, but doubts filled my mind as I ate. I was still sure that I could do something positive here, but wondered if I would ever come to enjoy running with Roy.

•

That night I slept a bone-weary sleep in the rudimentary accommodation offered at the park, my exhaustion overpowering a disturbing ache in my right knee. One of the symptoms of my ill-suitedness for suburban life had been an aversion to refrigerator ownership (something as big as a fridge felt like too much of a shackle to one place and while I had eventually caved in and got one, I'd never really reconciled myself to its presence); that night, however, I yearned for the ice that would normally be found in such an appliance. Why, at thirty-four, would I choose to put myself through this? I wondered. Who the hell is afraid of a fridge but ties themselves to a puma? My safari years were far enough behind me that I had reverted to my natural state—weak-kneed, soft-handed and fearful. I loved the philosophy of Inti Wara Yassi, but wasn't sure I had been very clever when I raised my hand to work with Roy. Then again, I'm a firm believer that the worst decisions often lead to the best adventures.

I got up at six am and dragged myself down the short stretch of road to the café where the volunteers gathered each morning before starting their day. Most of them were far younger than me, and bustled around with an energy I couldn't hope to muster at that hour of the morning without snorting instant coffee (something that should never be tried, even for a dare).

Some of the volunteers tended to capuchins, spider monkeys and squirrel monkeys that had been rehabilitated and released into the reserve but still needed some care and observation. Others looked after the monkeys that had only recently arrived and still required time in quarantine.

Some of the volunteers sitting around the breakfast table shouted like artillerymen, deafened perhaps by the parrots in their care. Then there were those who worked with the innocuous-sounding 'small animals', which included coatis, a relative of the raccoon with a short prehensile snout, and a badger-sized relative of the weasel called a tayra. While both these species are capable of displaying great affection to their carers, they are just as well known for turning savage and using their sharp teeth to inflict painful injuries.

By volunteering to spend time with Roy, I'd joined the last group at the table, the cat people. Oddly enough, my compatriots were openly envious of some of the wounds sported by the 'small animals' group: while no one was keen on pain, a scar did seem a great souvenir of this experience. The cats rarely bit hard enough to draw blood—not even Roy, who was the wildest of the four pumas at Machia. Mick's knee may have looked awful but his wounds were superficial and he had never needed a needle and thread to patch them up.

Despite this assurance, within two days I was able to show off some marks on my left knee, and I'd still not taken the cord, or lead, position. For reasons never explained, Roy liked to select just one knee on each of the volunteers who worked with him, and stuck to assaulting that knee alone, regardless of which was closest. Roy fancied my left.

When at last I took the cord position with Roy, I tried to hide my nerves while sweat that had naught to do with heat poured from my torso and brow. Despite knowing that Roy had never had a trainer he hadn't jumped, I thought I might become one of the people he jumped less often, for two reasons. Since I'd spent plenty of time with wild lions, leopards and cheetahs I felt sure I wouldn't be scared of him; I reasoned that Roy would pick up on my lack of fear and we'd become great friends. Also, I'd had a cat—called Tyson—during my previous few years in Australia. Tyson had died soon after my engagement ended, which was almost as big a blow as the loss of my human relationship. Foolishly, I was sure my understanding of a house cat would be at least partly transferable to a puma. I missed Tyson, and wanted that sort of relationship again. We'd be friends, Roy and me, just like Tyse and I had been, I was sure.

Sure.

Roy jumped me three times that first morning. Being tied to him naturally made me an easier target. No matter how many times I'd seen it happen to Mick and Adrian, there was nothing that could prepare me for the moment the puma stopped running then turned and faced me, pupils contracted, and launched himself lightning-fast at my left leg.

Pumas can bite much harder than Roy did, and inflict much more pain; nonetheless a primal part of me protested that what I was doing was silly and illogical. Some ancestral lizard inside me uncurled and squeaked at me to undo the rope, climb a tree, and stay away from anything large with fur and fangs. Let the puma run free!

But Roy could not be set free because, like many of the animals at Parque Machia and the three other parks run by Inti Wara Yassi, he was too young when he arrived to ever be able to survive in the wild. His mother had been killed, most likely for her skin, when Roy and his brother were far too young to fend for themselves. The strain of capture, confiscation and relocation had proved too much for Roy's brother and he had died soon after arriving at Parque Machia. Roy had thrived, though, and was renowned among the organisation's volunteers as the most demanding puma in any of Inti's parks. Demanding or not, he needed daily runs to maintain his health, and to give him a better quality of life than he would have if he was locked in a cage day after day.

'You *have* to keep him on the rope at all costs,' Mick had explained to me. 'He got off once, nobody will ever say how. Roy's a racist, hates Bolivians, and when he escaped, the first person he saw was a local guy. He took out the guy's spleen with a single swipe. If something like that ever happens again the place will be shut down and all these animals will just get sold off to zoos by the local council.'

'Right,' I thought now, determined to quash the impulse to release Roy. 'Keep him on the rope at all costs.'

The strain of running sixteen to twenty-five kilometres a day on difficult jungle terrain soon took its toll on my body. When Bondy had said Roy's handlers needed to be fit I'd believed I already was. Now I knew that was because I'd never been to a gym where the trainer bit you for running too slowly. Roy's handlers were perpetually soaked in sweat, a result of humidity so intense that breathing felt more like drowning. The closed-canopy rainforest under which we ran was stifling, yet in the rare moments we paused, it was quite beautiful. The air rang with the chatter of monkeys and clatter of woodpeckers, while crystal-clear streams ran off the peaks we tackled as part of Roy's daily routine.

'See that twitch?' said Mick one day after I'd been there about a week.

Roy's right foreleg had a definite quiver in it during one of his rare moments of inactivity; however, as predators are hardwired not to show weakness he did his best to hide it, even putting his full weight onto it to slow the tremor, in spite of the pain it obviously caused him.

'It's gonna need to be checked by one of the vets,' said Mick.

Roy wasn't due for his annual veterinary check-up for another month, but it had to be rescheduled for the following week so his leg could be examined properly.

Inti Wara Yassi, founded out of nothing by goodwill and run in the same way, is still a young organisation. It was founded and initially run by a man named Juan Carlos, a philanthropist who had already spent years taking in orphans and streetkids. These days its principal manager is a generous woman named Nina, whose colourful background includes a father who rode with Che Guevara. The only revolution Nina seeks though is a better life for Bolivia's animals. The whole organisation is held together by hope, a strong desire to do good, and bananas (lots of bananas), but very little money. An X-ray machine was as far out of Inti Wara Yassi's budget as a space shuttle, so Roy had to go to hospital. Without any veterinary hospitals within reasonable distance, there was only one place for him to go, a human hospital more than twenty kilometres away.

Unfortunately, another tool Inti Wara Yassi lacks is a vehicle.

•

'So, we're going in a taxi?' I asked, smiling, on the day of Roy's X-ray.

'*Si*,' replied one of the few permanent staff, a hard-working vet named Luis.

'Does the driver know that not all his passengers are human?' I asked.

'*Si*,' Luis said again, keeping to his pattern of not speaking English unless he had had a few drinks, then showing remarkable fluency.

So it was that Roy was anaesthetised and painstakingly manhandled down near-vertical drops and slippery-sloped trails on a stretcher. Along with two vets, plus Mick and Bondy (who'd decided it was too good a sight to miss), I clambered into the back of a station wagon taxi, its seats folded down to take the stretcher and its cargo. A small crowd drew around us, hoping to catch a glimpse of the famous Roy before we set off. (As well as the public, even other volunteers at Parque Machia are barred from visiting animals not in their care, so as to reduce the animals' exposure to humans.) The only person seemingly not impressed by Roy was the taxi driver, who acted as if this was nothing out of the ordinary and soon had us rumbling along the rutted road until we left the tar and hit an even janglier stretch of cobblestone, flanked by dank jungle.

After half an hour we came to a roadblock where teenaged soldiers were wielding machine guns—a fine incentive to stop. I wasn't sure what they were after—drugs, bribes, a hug?—but doubted we had the papers to prove we were legitimately permitted to transport a puma via taxi.

'Drug checkpoint,' Bondy said flatly.

I looked at Luis, who held a loaded syringe of anaesthetic low in his hand in case it should be needed, a bead of moisture glistening at its tip. 'Well, that doesn't look at all suspicious,' I thought. The soldiers approached with grim expressions, one holding something that looked a little like a corkscrew.

'They stick that thing into people's luggage and get a sample of what's inside,' Mick explained.

As they drew closer, the soldiers had a good look at the four people in the back of the taxi, but remained unaware of Roy, who was almost completely covered by a blanket. Only the tip of his tail was visible, occasionally twitching as he dreamt of chasing knees through a field.

As the soldiers stood beside the car with their sampling tool, Mick said calmly, 'Dare you to use it,' and whipped back the blanket. Roy's eyes were frozen open in the very same stare he used when about to attack, and both soldiers jumped back.

'Puma!' one of them exclaimed, quite unnecessarily.

In rapid-fire, urgent-sounding Spanish, Luis quickly explained our mission, and that we had to hurry as the puma could wake up at any moment and might become dangerous; he held up the syringe to emphasise his point.

The soldiers quickly waved us on. The look of mingled glee and excitement on their faces highlighted how young they were and how magnificent even a sleeping puma can be.

Finally arriving at the hospital after another half hour, we rushed Roy through the swinging doors, mindful as ever of his tail, then around a corner into a windowless corridor whose light fixtures had more blown bulbs than live ones.

We were met by a man wearing a beanie. He had a pair of glasses perched on his nose with lenses of such remarkable thickness that his neck must have felt the strain of the weight of them.

'*Radioliga*,' Luis said, and even with my limited Spanish I could guess at the man's profession.

We carefully lifted Roy off the stretcher, and laid him on the radiologist's table. His eyes were still wide open, and every now and then he would rumble through rubbery lips. The radiologist backed away, probably afraid, I thought, and wondered if he'd heard of Roy's reputation for de-spleening Bolivians. But then I heard a switch being flicked, followed by an indistinct buzzing. Glancing over, I was appalled to see the radiologist behind a screen, presumably lead, accompanied by a nurse. Surely they had heard of Marie Curie? Surely they should have warned us before releasing radioactive waves? The radiologist spoke to the vets, who repositioned Roy, and again with no preamble he flicked the switch. I was sure I felt hair growing on parts of my body where it had never grown before.

'Bloody hell,' Mick said. 'I think my nuts just shrank!'

It was only then that I noticed the radiologist was missing an arm from the elbow down. I nudged Bondy. 'Do you think he's met Roy before?'

We laughed, then the machine fired yet again and we left the room in a hurry, shooting spiteful glances at the one-armed man and covering our most delicate jewels as we went.

Once the plates were taken, the vets (who had stoically stayed in the room during the procedure) ushered us back in and we stretchered Roy out. News of his presence in the hospital had spread and a small crowd had gathered once again. Visitors, nurses, local children, and patients in vomit-green robes clustered in the hall. It was easy, if unfair, to be angry with Bolivians in general for what had been done to the animals that had ended up at the park, but these people showed a real awe at seeing Roy and I wondered if this was a small incidental opportunity to raise awareness of the need for puma preservation. It was impossible to know, but I was glad to be there, and waved as we all climbed into the back of the waiting taxi.

'*Ciao!*' a small child shouted cheerily, and soon the gathered crowd all started waving, calling '*ciao*' to the big cat they'd just seen.

As the taxi began to pull away I waved and called, '*Ciao!*'

'*Ciao!*' echoed Bondy. 'Meow!' shouted Mick.

Roy showed signs of waking on the ride back and was given another sedative. Though he was drugged the drive may still have been traumatic for him, but it was even more stressful for those of us wedged into a confined space with a puma who might wake at any time.

With slightly jangled nerves we arrived at the drug checkpoint again. There were more soldiers than before, and we were waved away from the other cars towards a sinister-looking section out of sight of the road. A soldier with more stripes than the others approached the taxi, followed by his minions. 'Bugger,' I thought, 'we're in trouble.' Paperwork could take hours in a place like this— hours and perhaps bribes that none of us had.

The officer pulled back the blanket that covered Roy, gave a 'hmmph' of triumph, then turned and spoke in Spanish to his assembled men. One of the soldiers whipped a small camera out of his pocket, and the officer quickly struck a pose beside Roy's form, had his portrait taken, said '*Gracias*,' and signalled us to drive on.

I learnt later that the region of Bolivia where Parque Machia is located is, after Ecuador and Peru, the third-largest coca-growing area in the world. The drug checkpoint we'd encountered on the way to and from the hospital was a permanent fixture, required if the country was to continue receiving US aid dollars. However, since it was known to everyone in the area and beyond, it was about as effective as fish-scented deodorant.

Unfortunately, the local coca growers, supported by the mayor, had started to build an illegal road around the checkpoint, bulldozing a swathe through the jungle, even toppling trees onto an enclosure where monkeys were being rehabilitated. If completed, the road had the potential to shut down Parque Machia altogether. By law, the mayor would then be in a position to dictate which animals were moved to other reserves and which stayed. As the tourists who came to the area often expressed dismay that they were not allowed near the pumas or ocelots, undoubtedly the mayor would want to keep some of these animals. Without the Inti Wara Yassi volunteers to walk them every day, they would need to be kept in cages. Ominously, only the rainy season was holding back the completion of the coca growers' road.

•

The results of the X-ray revealed that Roy was suffering from a serious calcium deficiency, most likely congenital.

'Man, his bones looked like a bird's,' said Rob, a Californian animal lover who donated several months of each year to Inti Wara Yassi, and who had known Roy for years. He'd become something of an expert on captive big cats. Rob and the vets devised a plan to supplement Roy's daily diet of chicken and beef with calcium powder. This had to be smeared all over Roy's food each day, a revolting job for me, Adrian, Mick and any future Roy Boys.

'I'm not sure I want him getting any stronger,' I said to Adrian as we trudged up the trail to Roy's enclosure one morning. The path still left me panting, despite the fitness I was gaining daily.

'Me neither, but you know something?' said Adrian. 'Now that I know Roy isn't well I feel a bit differently towards him. I'm not so angry with him when he's being a bastard.'

I wished I felt the same way. But contrary to my hope of forming a special connection with the puma, it had become apparent that I was a target for Roy's aggression. He was known to jump some people more than others—and I had turned out to be one of those people. I held no dislike for Roy, but no affection either. I just wanted to make it through each day, getting jumped on as little as possible.

When I first arrived there I'd considered staying longer than four weeks at Parque Machia, maybe even settling in this patch of Bolivian jungle for a few months. But after dealing with Roy for a while I just wanted to get through the time I'd signed on for, to prove to myself that I couldn't be beaten by a girly-faced, chicken-boned, racist cat.

Don't Eat My Hero

Parque Machia was in a state of nervous anticipation, the entire place humming with activity. We were expecting a famous visitor, someone well known to anyone with more than a passing interest in wildlife: Dame Jane Goodall, whose research into chimpanzees has changed the way we think about apes, ourselves, and how wildlife research is conducted, was visiting the reserve for a night. Accompanying her would be the founder of Inti Wara Yassi, Juan Carlos, and some of the orphans and homeless children in his charge.

While others did their best to buff and polish surfaces—which the monkeys immediately befouled—Mick and I took Roy out for his morning round. Mick was leaving the park in the next few days, and wanted to spend as much time with Roy as possible. Adrian was thrilled to have a day off the trail which he could spend lazing at the tourist aviary, a dull job but one that involved no hills or bites—unless you were outwitted by a macaw.

I was in lead position, which meant the rope went directly from Roy's collar to my waist, with sturdy carabiners holding it in place at both ends. Though the rope was ten metres long, it was never willingly fed out to full length, and my aim was to keep it coiled in my left hand with a little over a metre granted to Roy for most of the walk, more when we went down steep hills, much less as we approached his 'hot zones', as we called his regular, inexplicable-to-all-but-him places of attack. Mick stayed as close to my heels as he could without tripping me, close enough that if Roy did jump me he would be there straightaway to lead him off once I had dislodged his claws.

The walk started well; I even thought that after two weeks maybe Roy was getting used to me, and perhaps I was getting better at judging his moods and reading his body language, anticipating his jumps and sliding my hand down the rope close to the collar to block his turns. My knee still suffered regular abuse, but not as often as at the start of my tenure. So it was with confidence that I tackled one of the toughest parts of the trail, which involved dropping a full body length onto a narrow ledge, then immediately leaping onto a well-polished log that traversed a sheer rock face, using the momentum to jump again onto moderately firmer ground. This was followed directly by a run and jump onto a rock, requiring a well-timed grab at a tree to stop sliding down a ledge. Three paces later came a tight squeeze between two vertical rock faces, made worse by the slippery surface underfoot where water pooled. This was one of the first times I remembered to get close to Roy straight after the gap: this was important as he always attempted a left turn at that point, even though the trail went right.

'Pete? Mick?' came a voice ahead of us.

Roy instantly froze, his ears swinging forward and locking. The voice belonged to Bec, who worked with a puma named Sonko. Sonko was fat, and Roy Boys delighted in pointing out his bulk, not so subtly hinting that Roy was the *real* puma. As well as being fat, Sonko squeaked like a baby alligator. People who worked with Sonko invariably claimed Roy was a bit soft. Which he wasn't. He was just pretty. Nevertheless, a rivalry existed between Sonko's handlers and the Roy Boys, and insults were often exchanged.

'Yep?' Mick shouted back.

'Sonko is lying down, hasn't moved for half an hour,' Bec called to us now.

'Kick him!' shouted Mick.

Sonko's volunteers treated Mick's suggestion with the disdain it deserved, and we were at an impasse. Pumas are solitary by nature and two male pumas never get together casually to discuss sport or girls. They only come together to fight for land. The two pumas' trails overlapped in many places, and the points where they crossed almost flowed with the urine unleashed by these two alpha males as they felt the need to counter the territorial markings of the other. For Roy and Sonko to meet could be catastrophic, so we needed to do something—fast.

Roy, Mick and I stood at the top of a steep gully with smooth river rocks at its base. The other river bank had more vegetation, but not too far up it linked with our trail again. If we cut down the bank then scrambled up the other side, somehow coaxing Roy ahead of us, we would overtake Sonko without the pumas coming face to face.

I turned Roy back in the very direction I'd just denied him, and his pace immediately picked up. Every day he aimed for this route, and every day he was refused. As we reached the river bank he moved even faster, and my boots scrabbled for purchase on the moss-covered, rounded rocks. Roy's four points on the ground made him far more sure-footed than me, not to mention that he had evolved for such terrain and I have a noted lack of coordination.

'Try to steer him up the bank here,' called Mick, but the rope had played out, and swinging my arm to the right barely influenced Roy's path.

Roy continued on faster still, and with no way of slowing him down I was forced to let out more rope, even though over half of its length had already slid painfully through my palm. To this point the river bed was level, but ahead was a downward slope, and a trail used by some of Inti's other animals.

Then, over the sounds of jungle insects and the ever-present, strangely electronic burbling of a type of bird called an oropendola, came a sound I hadn't imagined hearing here. It was children singing. *It was the orphans singing to Jane Goodall!* I realised, struck by a sudden horrifying vision of meeting the woman who'd been my hero since I was a boy, and Roy biting her or some child that fate had already mistreated. I upped my pace considerably, trying to catch up to Roy so I could grab his collar, Mick still right behind me even though the going was now just as tough for him.

But Roy was faster, and hit the slope at a sprint, his intent ominous. The rope pulled tight, and even though Roy weighed less than me I was pulled clean off my feet, landing face down and head first before being dragged sideways, injuriously to both pride and skin. By now, Roy was already over the crest of the hill, and as I reached it I clutched at a wrist-thick tree, gripping with all the strength of my left hand and yanking us to a halt.

I looked down the slope at Roy, who glanced back, his face set in the expression that meant he was about to cause mayhem. He jerked his body sideways with such incredible strength that the tree, still in my grip, was torn from the ground, and then he started dragging me along again. The sensation was like being dumped by a wave, but without the cushioning softness of water. I was smashed against rocks, bounced over stumps, and burnt by the friction of dirt and sharp grass tussocks. My body was soon so battered that I had no idea which part of it suddenly connected with a rock and somehow, mercifully, bounced me upright for a brief moment.

I took a running step but immediately lost my balance again, the rope at my waist yanking me at an odd angle. To my right was a tree, this one far larger than the one I'd grabbed previously, probably about the thickness of a telegraph pole. Grabbing it one-handed was out of the question, so with the last iota of strength available to me I launched at it bodily, hoping to plaster myself like a skydiving koala against its rough bark. As with many of my athletic endeavours, I missed the mark and sailed wide. However, this left the rope bent around the trunk in a U, with Roy's momentum on one side and mine on the other. For once my weight counted, and Roy's advance was brought to a crashing halt as the rope pulled tight, while I was slammed against the tree, causing sharp and sudden pain to my wrist and other areas. I fell to the ground again, using the tree and my heft as a brake, and watched Mick run past me to calm and collect Roy.

Before I could decide not to, I stood up. Wincing, spitting out dirt, I joined Mick and the still wide-eyed Roy.

'You can walk?' Mick asked, genuinely incredulous.

'Since I was about a year old, actually,' I replied, most likely in shock.

'I was sure you must have broken something.'

'Not sure that I haven't.'

In fact, I thought it might just be adrenalin keeping me upright, but I wanted to get Roy away from the orphans before that could be confirmed.

It turned out that my misadventure had resulted in only bruises, abrasions and welts, and I was well enough to attend the dinner in honour of Jane that evening. I put on a now unaccustomed shirt so

Jane wouldn't have to see the damage I'd incurred in attempting to protect her, but she seemed grateful when I told her, in as offhand a tone as I could manage, of the day's events. She appeared tired, not surprising considering she is in her seventies and still travels three hundred days of the year to promote conservation.

Right then and there, talking to Jane, I decided that complaining about bumps and bruises was fine, but that it was time to stop worrying about my age. In fact, if I'd learnt anything it was that getting older was great. I had enough experience to put what I'd learnt from life into practice, could laugh at myself more comfortably than ever before, and had as much fun as when I was a teen. It was ageing that was a bastard, but while my knees held out and my lungs drew air I would make sure to enjoy every moment I spent being beaten up by a half-wild puma, because it was so much better than being beaten down by a desk.

Dressed for a Kill

The next day was Mick's last with Roy, and he took the cord for the whole day. I filmed much of it, hoping to give him a memento of one of Roy's jumps besides the light scarring on his mangled right knee. But Roy behaved like a kitten, not even attempting an attack, just trotting mellowly and politely along the trails, responding with affection whenever Mick drew close. (Roy, like all cats, showed he liked you by bumping his head against yours—not fun if it's an English soccer fan, only marginally more so with a puma.)

At the end of the afternoon walk, Mick said goodbye to Roy, ending his heroically long six-week stint with him. Mick's eyes were watery as he walked away, but I didn't feel like even gently mocking him. In truth, I was perplexed by his apparent love for this ill-tempered animal.

I had loved many animals in the past, more than I could count, but apart from the benign contact of pets (none of them larger than Bunty the sheep) it had always been at a distance. I knew that the lions and elephants I'd observed daily in Botswana might kill me if I approached them, but they would never hurt you out of malice; they don't recognise that we *feel*, so they can't intentionally inflict pain or fear. In fact, it was their wildness that appealed to me. Roy was different—not a pet, but nor was he exactly wild. I couldn't shake the feeling that his aggression was deliberate, vindictive even. Learning to enjoy it would not be easy.

With Mick gone, Adrian and I kept running with Roy, hoping a suitable candidate would soon appear to help us out. Meanwhile, with no one to give us a rest, we had to slog through day after day, a punishing ordeal, made worse by the foul mood Roy seemed to have fallen into since Mick left. He was jumping us at every hot zone, and quite often in areas outside them as well. Each morning Adrian and I would sit at breakfast shooting shifty glances at the clock that seemed to be moving too fast towards the hour when we would have to face the walk to Roy's cage, braced for violence and pain. One day Roy bit me a record four times, and made another six attempts I was able to block, making me seriously wonder why I ever signed up for this. The notion of doing good seemed faint, and I wondered whether all those who'd called me a fool might not be correct.

•

'This place sucks,' said Jodie, an American girl who worked in the monkey quarantine area, across the lunch table one day. 'They have too many animals, and hardly any get released. It sucks,' she said again, taking an aggressive drag of her cigarette.

Characteristically, even though she was giving voice to some of my own feelings, as soon as I heard them I felt the need to argue.

'It does if you think that the sole aim is to release animals,' I replied. 'But most injured wild animals die. And most of the ones brought here to Inti have injuries too severe for the animal to ever be released again, or they have no habitat to return to. If they're not going to be locked in a cage or euthanased, giving them the best possible life they can have is the only option.'

Jodie nodded, reluctantly agreeing, and I continued on enthusiastically, inspiring myself. 'If at the end of the day you can believe that one animal's life is better, even if just for that day, because of what you have done, then why not be happy with that?'

She nodded again, and so did I, having managed to convince myself as much as her. We both knew that Inti would never refuse an animal care, and that we were doing everything we could for every one. Roy wasn't to blame for the way he behaved. Inti Wara Yassi couldn't afford trainers for the animals; their only aim was for Roy, the monkeys, Baloo the bear, the birds and the nasty small animals to be as wild as they could be given that they couldn't be wild. It was flawed, but noble.

'Bloody hell,' I thought suddenly, 'flawed but noble pretty much describes Roy too.'

This epiphany made me feel renewed somewhat, and that afternoon I approached Roy with a different attitude. It wasn't his fault that his mother had been killed, and I couldn't blame him for wanting to be wild and puma-like. I should embrace it, embrace it all—the charging, the bites, the rolling around to gain more rope so he could jump me, and the awkward moments when he stared into my eyes while defecating. Roy's behaviour often felt malicious to me, but I knew better, knew enough not to anthropomorphise him, knew enough now to appreciate him as a puma. I just had to try to remember this each time he latched onto my leg.

The afternoon's walk went well, with only a few half-hearted jump attempts. It was most likely a coincidence, but I felt as though Roy and I had made a breakthrough.

Things seemed to be looking up even more when Adrian and I were granted a trainee. Once we'd trained the new Roy Boy—which would take at least four days—we could start having the occasional day off. My mood was heading towards buoyant. With a day's break I might just make it through the remaining two weeks of my stay.

That night there was a party for the volunteers, and I let myself go more than a little with a nasty local brew called Singani, made primarily of cane sugar and Satan's urine (at least that was the theory I developed in my throbbing head the next day).

I hoped it was just my alcohol-addled ears deceiving me when I heard what sounded like an auction starting, but next thing I knew the item being bid for was me.

'Wha . . . ?' I said eloquently.

Bondy, who was acting as auctioneer, kindly explained: the Roy Boys' services were for sale to the other volunteers. Being stupid or macho enough to volunteer to run with Roy made us the perfect victims. The money raised would be put towards caring for the animals.

I mumbled something about my discomfort at being sold as a slave when I already suffered daily indignities at the paws of Roy and the trail itself, but had no real recourse.

The bids climbed, admittedly at the pace of a sloth, and I watched nervously as a Swiss girl of volatile temperament took the lead. She was predatory in her approach to men, and possibly had teeth in intriguing places, and I was worried that she might not accept there were some things I wouldn't do, even for charity.

To my enormous relief a coalition formed to challenge her bid, and I was ultimately sold to a group of four girls, who immediately set about devising their plan for me in the twenty-four-hour period I would be their slave.

Adrian was also sold, and I watched his face deflate like a balloon when the Swiss girl made the winning bid.

'Bad luck, mate,' I consoled. 'Can't imagine the demands I get will be as bad as yours.'

First up for me during my twenty-four hours of slavery was cooking dinner, something I thought might well be more hazardous for the girls than for me as the only thing worse than my cooking ability was the choice of local ingredients. I had some desultory-looking vegetables, a disturbingly yellow-fleshed chicken, some curry powder and oil that looked less like that from an olive and more like that from an engine. Massages were also ordered and performed.

Then came the clincher. In keeping with the intended attack on the Roy Boys' machismo—and being macho is not something I'm often accused of; in fact, as a soft Sydneysider I am so in touch with my feminine side it would be no surprise if I lactated—I was required, purely for my owners' amusement, to wear a dress. And not just any dress. The small town adjacent to the reserve had a store selling second-hand and fancy-dress clothes, from which a pink and white chequered schoolgirl's dress had been selected. It was garish, and tight in all the wrong places.

'I think we need to talk about rugby a lot today,' I said as I emerged in my gorgeous attire to the jeers and hoots of the other volunteers.

The new trainee, an Englishman named John, was starting with us that day. I began to explain to him some of Roy's quirks, but he soon interrupted me. 'You know I can't really take in anything you're saying while you're wearing that, right?'

'Right,' I said. 'Adrian, maybe you better go over it all. I'll just go machete some vines or something.'

Maybe Roy felt some smug satisfaction at seeing me in a dress ('Who's got feminine features now?' I could imagine him asking), but like most animals he wasn't interested in clothing unless it smelled peculiar. He greeted us the same way he did every morning, and eyed John the trainee with a look I'd seen before.

'Let's see what sort of mood he's in,' I said as we approached the first hill on Roy's trail. 'Keep up if you can, John,' I added, just as Roy bolted.

By now, Adrian and I were used to the footholds, and knew which trees you could grab and which you couldn't. (With no guide to the area's flora, we had come up with our own names for some distinctive species, including the Bastard Tree, covered in vicious spines usually concealed under beards of lichen. You only grabbed a Bastard Tree once.) John didn't know the trail, and I heard him cursing in his English accent and a solid 'thwap' at one point as he slipped, but I had no time to turn as Roy was putting on a show and ran, ran and ran.

'Not good,' Adrian said simply.

Roy barely paused until we approached one of his hot zones, at which stage I became anxious that he was just getting his energy levels back up for some hard jumping.

He was. I wasn't on lead, so Adrian took the brunt of it, but as the number-two guy my job was to be there and make sure that I got Roy off him fast, then lead him away until we were out of the area. But the moment I had him off Adrian he jumped me. Adrian pulled him off—and he went straight for Adrian again. We finally got him through the zone and had some respite for the next few minutes as he kept a pace just above leisurely.

Once he had the breath to speak, Adrian added to his earlier verdict: 'Not good at all.' I grunted my agreement, and trotted along behind him, offering words of encouragement to John, who was struggling to keep up with us.

'Frankly I think it's lunatic to go out every day into the jungle when there's a very good chance that a puma will bite you,' said John at the end of the walk. 'I think you're both mad.'

'I don't suppose I can argue with that while wearing this,' I said, plucking at the stifling inbuilt lycra knickers of my outfit with one hand, and reaching for the machete with the other, in the hope of looking more butch.

'You look like Braveheart's gay cousin,' John commented.

I was worried that John might quit, and leave us without a substitute. Two days later he did, limping off with a sprained ankle, and once again it was just the three of us on the trails, Adrian and me plagued by fatigue and footrot, Roy unfazed by anything except when we managed to block his attempts in the hot zones.

Soon afterwards we had a scorchingly hot day, the sort that raises beads of sweat on your brow at the mere thought of action. Despite the knowledge that we'd perspire so profusely that it would stream down our legs and fill our boots, Adrian and I liked these days. The trail was exhausting enough for us in these conditions, but Roy had to do it wearing a fur coat. He generally ran little on these days, taking the shortest trails and, most welcome of all, jumping far less than usual.

True to form, though, Roy defied our expectations and took off early, maintaining a punishing pace. My feet squelched in their rubber tombs, and mosquitoes, trying to bite me, instead drowned in the rivers of sweat that flowed over my body.

Roy kept running and eventually we crossed a particularly slippery part of the trail, sliding and skidding to keep up before dropping down to one of the most picturesque sections. It was a creek bed with a series of small falls and crystal-clear pools. Ferns acted as parasols overhead and the jungle rang with constant cries of alarm from monkeys as Roy passed through. Roy would often stop to drink here, and on some days pause for a rest, settling gently into one of the pools.

Today the heat had finally taken its toll on him and he decided to linger for a dip. I gently scooped up some water into my hands and trickled it over his head and ears until he flicked his tail, letting me know he'd had enough.

The sound of a small motor approached, incongruous in such a setting. On occasion we heard trucks on the nearby roads as they carried their loads of lumber (and with it the sad promise of more habitat loss and therefore stranded animals) to the nearby mill, but this was a different noise. Then suddenly, from down the creek came a flash of green and purple, zigging beelike before zagging away, almost too fast to see. Finally the hummingbird came closer, and to my utter delight it hovered, wings whirring and making the mechanical sound within inches of Roy's head, directly over his upturned face. It held itself there then scooted to Adrian, where it paused briefly, before repeating the performance with me, fanning my face with manic wingbeats. Then with a whirr of wings and a pop of colour it was gone. It was such a rare moment, something so hard to explain, so beautiful and wonderful and unexpected. A jewel in time.

'Wow,' I said, to Roy, to Adrian, to myself.

'Nice,' said Adrian.

Even though Roy usually showed his hunting instincts by flushing out and chasing ground birds on the trail, he didn't react to the hummingbird at all. He just stood up, shook himself like a dog, spraying Adrian and me in the process, and set off again, refreshed enough that he made a half-hearted jump just along the trail. But my mood couldn't be dampened, and I felt an unfamiliar flicker of enjoyment.

'Good boy,' I said to Roy, and to my surprise, I meant it.

The Last Temptation of Roy

Over the next few days something strange happened: Roy's hot zones went cold. At the approach to each hot zone an anticipatory noise like the zinging of violins would start in my ears, but Roy just strolled on through, not even glancing back at us to see if we were lagging behind enough for him to wreak havoc. Normally he was diligent in checking our whereabouts during the hot zones—if we weren't right by his shoulders and ready to grab his collar he rarely missed an opportunity to turn and bite.

Each day someone would ask Adrian and me how Roy was behaving. His reputation at the park was that of the adventure cat, but for two and a half days we had to disappoint them by replying, 'He's turned into a puppy. Just quietly walks the trails.' I started patting him when I had the chance, and even bent down and bumped heads with him on occasion, smiling when he returned the gesture. It was as if I had passed a test, and we now had a bond impossible to imagine two weeks before. Whether all the early jumping had been intended to assert dominance, or to try to drive me away, I couldn't know. Regardless, I was glad for the reprieve, and spoke to Roy in softer tones, using the word 'bastard' a lot less often when talking about him to the other volunteers.

But of course it couldn't last.

There was a section of Roy's trail I'd long dreaded, for two reasons. At that point the trail split, and Roy could choose to take a long detour, extending the punishment of our daily routine by several kilometres. Thre was also a sharp drop in the trail at this point, which required perfect timing and great balance for a human to negotiate, two things genetics sadly withheld from me. To handle the drop I had to make sure I was right behind Roy, because he managed it with ease and then tended to take off at a sprint as soon as he touched the ground. If the rope pulled tight while I was in mid-air I was likely to be pasted onto a tree—again. Failing that, I would often launch off the drop weak-limbed, landing floppily, and miss the tree a metre or so down the path that could be used as an anchor.

While missing this tree usually just led to some mad skating, uncoordinated cartwheeling of legs, and inelegant flailing at imaginary handholds until I collided with the next tree on the path, on this day my feet shot forward from under me and I landed heavily on my backside. The ground was muddy and slippery from the previous evening's rain, and I soon began an uncontrolled slide down the trail. Sometime during this slide, my shorts split at the seam. Roy had stopped his initial sprint and settled into a fast walk when he saw movement beside him. It was me, sliding right past him—a scene way too tempting for any puma to ignore.

'Hi Roy!' I said in as even a tone as I could muster with my shorts torn open, mud filling my underpants, and a puma eyeing me in delight. Naturally, he jumped on me.

Roy's teeth on my leg stopped my slide, but due to my prone position he hit me higher than usual, the thigh rather than the knee. I quickly realised how much more painful a tooth into muscle is than a tooth into bone. Usually when he bit me I would maintain a calm voice, so as not to excite him further. But unable to manage such self-control, I shouted out something that is rude in most languages, and shoved at Roy's head; however, with my leg flat to the ground I was unable to remove his paws.

Adrian rushed up and grabbed the lead, allowing me to stand up and remove Roy's paws. As he did so often after jumping, Roy sprinted, and only then did I see that there was barely a metre of free cord between Roy and me, the rest having somehow coiled itself around Roy's body. Yanked out of Adrian's hand the rope pulled tight, but I was already running. Roy turned, frustrated at my slow pace, and jumped me again. Thunder cracked overhead, drowning out my curses (by now I'd completely forgotten about remaining calm). This time he hit me low, pushing me over, which sent us both into a spin during which one of his claws dragged down my calf, taking my boot off with it.

Adrian caught up to us in record time, and grabbed at Roy's cord, managing to free one loop that had formed around his body. The other loops pulled tight though and I found myself being dragged by a half-crazed puma once again. Soon, frustrated at the shortness of the cord, Roy turned to jump on me again, but this time I nabbed his collar and dragged him along the path, loosening the coils of rope from the various places they were wrapped around him.

My three-quarter-length shorts had started the day in no way mistakable for couture, but by now they were shredded, the seat flapping, the section below the left knee hanging by threads. It was one of the few times that Roy had drawn blood, and I could see a small bloom of red through the remaining fabric.

'Roy didn't like me falling over. He seems to blame my leg,' I said, as thunder rumbled again.

A breeze kicked up and Adrian and I both checked the glimpses of sky through the canopy while keeping pace with our perturbed puma. Black clouds had gathered overhead, and an ominous swirling of foliage made it impossible to ignore that a drenching was on its way. We'd been rained on before—only natural in a rainforest—but the heaviest rains of the year were due to start soon, and this was setting out to be a potent warm-up act. Roy's fur stood on end as if electrified, and with the next crash of thunder he glanced back at us with an expression that suggested he thought the sound was our fault. Specifically, my knee's.

As the first fat splats of rain hit the canopy above, then burst through in a torrent, it became obvious that as far as Roy was concerned, yes, the rain *was* my knee's fault. After nearly three days of casual and pleasant trails I had been jumped three times in half an hour, and was starting to feel my existing wounds tugged in uncomfortable directions. The pelting rain made the trail slippery even for four-legged Roy, a plus, but for the first time on one of our trails I felt cold.

Then I saw Roy shiver. He curtailed it as quickly as he could, but the shiver made him seem a little vulnerable. While I wouldn't have dared admit to it outside the small circle of Roy Boys, at that moment his attempt at bravado was just a tiny bit cute.

'Bloody hell,' I thought, 'he's just bitten me three times but I think I'm starting to like him even more!' The temporary break from violence had allowed me to feel closer to him, and somehow the return of his abusive behaviour didn't change that. Since I'd stopped focusing on my own pain and stopped blaming Roy for it, I could see that Roy jumped merely because he was excitable. He loved these walks, and had no way of expressing himself other than by being a puma. He was more trapped between worlds than I had ever been, and could not be blamed for behaving wildly.

The rain dissipated within a day, leaving behind treacherously slippery trails that even Roy took slowly. By now Adrian and I were exhausted, battered, and plagued with the strange rashes that come from being constantly wet. Our feet emerged from their boots each day prune-like and peeling, a ghastly white and sore to the touch. We were near the end of our month at Parque Machia, and both of us were keen to move on to somewhere else. We needed trainees, new Roy Boys.

By a happy quirk of fate, within two days two new potential candidates arrived; following a trend, they were both Australians.

'So do you guys pat him?' asked Courtney, one of the new trainees.

'Not so much,' Adrian answered.

'Hmmph,' said Courtney, and I knew that just like me a month earlier, he was imagining that by the end of his stint he would have Roy on a string, and that they would have become great buddies. The truth is that I did pat Roy, but not often, and only when we were in the safest areas. Affection usually generated excitement, and excitement led to jumping, so love was limited between us, even with the new respect and fonder feelings I had for Roy.

'Just so you know,' I explained, remembering my own earlier arrogance, 'if you've ever owned a cat and therefore think you know how to handle a puma, you don't. It would be like playing with sharks because you once owned a goldfish.'

It only took Courtney one turn on lead to shake his confidence. Roy's crazy face was unsettling enough, but just like me, Courtney wasn't prepared for the shock of actually being bitten by a puma.

And Roy went after him, jumping him often and with a degree of venom I didn't recall experiencing during my own training, only a month before.

'You know what,' said Courtney after a few days. 'I'm not interested in being his buddy anymore. I just want to make it through the month.'

I grinned broadly at this. Courtney looked at me questioningly, so I explained that I'd experienced exactly what he was going through, and presumably so had any number of Roy Boys through the seven years Roy had been at Machia.

I left Machia just as the rains arrived, coming down with a fury as they had on the day when everything was my knee's fault. I was glad to get out before the rains hit too hard, making the trails unmanageable, but I also felt wistful to be leaving when I'd only just begun to have fun with Roy. I had started to respect as well as like him: he was a real puma.

There were other reasons for my regret, too. No longer at the mercy of his attacks, all I could think of was how vulnerable Roy was. I had no idea how much time Parque Machia would remain running before the drug growers' road—stemming from the desire for cocaine in far parts of the world—shut it down. And I worried whether the supply of Roy Boys, never strong, could continue to trickle on. Strange as it would have seemed to me only a week before, on the day I left it wasn't just raindrops wetting my cheeks.

Not the End of the World

After returning to the Gomezes' house to recover from Roy's attentions and rediscover the joys of Marguerite's pisco sours, I found myself needing to recuperate from those beverages as well. This took me to not-too-distant Buenos Aires, where I had a wonderful reunion with my sister, Laurie, who was visiting Argentina from Australia. I also met Laurie's friends Freddy and his wife, who invited us to dinner at their house in Buenos Aires, an occasion that inadvertently led me to the destination for my next journey.

'Do you think Argentina is more like Switzerland or Ethiopia?' Freddy asked at some stage of the evening.

I thought of the famous story of the Argentinian football players stranded after a plane crash who resorted to cannibalism in the bitter cold, I thought of condors soaring over the high Andes, I thought of fine Argentinian wine and the slopes where the grapes grew. Switzerland seemed the obvious answer, but even on our short acquaintance Freddy struck me as the sort of person who enjoyed trick questions, so I chose Ethiopia.

'Exactly!' was Freddy's delighted reply. 'Most of Argentina is desert—dry, horrible desert, barely worth farming. Only in the east and right at the south do you have mountains and snow. The south, Patagonia, that's what a lot of people think Argentina is like. There it is cold, with high mountains, condors soaring, day-long sun . . . but that is only in Patagonia.'

By this stage the scars on my knee had faded enough that it looked like I'd been attacked by nothing more savage than acne, and I was keen to have a new adventure. Freddy's description made me determined to visit Patagonia, a region of southern Argentina and Chile.

In travellers' circles and in some literature, Patagonia is famous for its stark landscapes, bleak winds, peaks capped with year-round snow, and the largest sheet of ice outside the polar regions. Few animals survive there, but I thought I might be able to find pumas (something I now had mixed feelings about), penguins, seals and orcas. (Orca is the new name for killer whales, though I doubt the recent name change has altered their temperament.)

Patagonia also seemed to have a reputation as being one of the destinations of choice for those looking to have their soul shaken, or to find out if they have one. In the early 1800s Charles Darwin visited the island of Tierra del Fuego and reported seeing no structures, just the fires after which the island was named. He said the people were barely human; the most primitive he had ever seen. While I thought his comments about the people were needlessly unkind (and ignored how advanced they must have had to be to survive in such a place), I hoped that in Patagonia I would feel the wildness for which it is famous.

•

As soon as Laurie returned to Australia, I headed south to the Chilean town of Puerto Montt to take a flight to the furthermost reaches of Patagonia. I'd settled on Ushuaia on the island of Tierra del Fuego as my first destination. Proudly proclaimed by its residents as the world's southernmost city, Ushuaia's position in the south of Patagonia also made it a likely place to see condors close up.

My entrance into Ushuaia—flying in through a cleft in jagged, white-capped mountains—made me feel uncharacteristically opti-mistic. Nowhere I'd been in Africa looked remotely like this, and as an Australian I am easily impressed by mountains (the tallest peak in Australia requires a comparative stroll to reach its summit). The mountains around Ushuaia looked not just untrammelled, but untrammellable. Which is clearly not a real word, but was a very real feeling.

Walking through Ushuaia's airport, I saw a tourist shop with a sign declaring it to be 'The store at the end of the world at the airport at the end of the world', something I thought a wee bit tacky. Then again, I long ago learnt the old adage 'Never judge a place by its airport'.

By the time I got to San Martin, the main drag of Ushuaia, I was wondering if Charles Darwin would have been even harsher on the place if he'd visited today, since at least the locals he'd been so unkind about hadn't tried to sell him anything. Hawkers squawked outside every bar and restaurant, trying to entice passers-by with dinner deals and happy-hour specials. I soon discovered that Ushuaia saw a lot of cruise passengers who stayed in town for only a few hours before heading on to Antarctica. The cruise-goers appeared in town soon after gangways were lowered, rolling down the street like a human tsunami dressed in yellow and red windproof parkas and tassled hats. There was a whiff of desperation in some of the stores, which flogged Argentinian soccer jerseys, *mate* (the local tea) and its associated tea-making paraphernalia, addictive local red wine, and miniature dolls dressed in the costumes of cultures either long gone or waning.

Two nights into my stay in Ushuaia, I was sitting in the common area of a backpackers' hostel—the sort of accommodation I would use throughout my South American journey, even though I would often be the oldest person there—talking to a young German called Friederike. I'd been expressing my dissatisfaction with Ushuaia when Friederike said, 'Maybe you've travelled too much. Perhaps you are too hard to impress now. I worry the same will happen to me.'

'Maybe she's right,' I thought, and wondered if I'd been as wise as her at twenty-one (I suspect not). Maybe I was just too old for this near-hobo existence, I reflected yet again. But I had not been very successful in any field except guiding, and even that I had given up.

Despite such misgivings, I did have someone to look up who—thankfully—had no interest in hawking me a boat cruise, rental bicycle, or 'end of the world' snow dome. Freddy's wife had a zoologist niece called Marcella who was in Ushuaia studying the breeding habits of Chilean swallows. Marcella took me on some of the many daytrips I made from Ushuaia in search of the overwhelming sense of isolation and wildness that the guidebooks described. She didn't seem to mind me squelching along behind her as she checked the nests of Chilean swallows, which always seemed to be in a bog. Marcella was there to collect breeding data. This was as far south as any species of swallow went, so for them at least this really was the end of the world.

Walking in the bogs one day, I asked Marcella what the main source of employment for Ushuaians was. I'd learnt Ushuaia had a population of roughly twenty thousand people, not all of whom could possibly be in the trinket business, even if it felt that way.

'Construction,' Marcella replied, expertly plucking a newly hatched Chilean swallow from its nesting box. Unlike the adult plumage of muted grey underneath and dark blue above, this hatchling was pink and naked. Marcella blew on it to keep it warm, before dropping it into a small plastic bag, weighing it, marking a claw with nail polish, and returning it to its feathered sanctuary before repeating the process with one of its nestmates.

'Oh,' I said, a little perplexed. 'Constructing what?'

'Hotels mainly.' We tramped through the bog to the next nest box she was monitoring. Mud splashed high up her rubber boots, and straight over the low tops of mine and into my socks, a reminder that I was maybe not quite prepared for this place. 'And shops for the tourists,' she added after she was done with the next batch of chicks.

'But the tourists come on boats and usually stay on board. What do they need hotels for?' I asked, making a futile attempt to shake mud from my boot and spattering my other leg in the process.

There was a pause as Marcella inspected another nest. 'Southern house wren,' she said, and I thought she was being cryptic until I realised she was waiting for me to jot that down on a sheet next to the corresponding nest-box number.

'The hotels are for the tourists the council hopes will come,' Marcella carried on. 'They need jobs for all the people now that the television factory has shut down.'

It seemed incomprehensibly odd to me that there had ever been a television-making industry in this far-flung place, an entire continent away from regular shipping routes since the Panama Canal had been built (which had happened well before television, I was pretty sure) and in a country not otherwise known for its electronics. But there it was, the television factory had supported Ushuaia from the 1960s to the late 1990s. I found myself imagining the industry as a cover for the sort of villain who appears in James Bond films; perhaps one of the nearby mountains had concealed their underground lairs at the end of the world. Then again, those villains liked their comforts. This place was just too cold.

Incredibly, despite the bitter winds sending a chill through me whenever I ventured outside, this was summer. And not just summer, but high summer. Yet snow still topped the mountains and no sensible person would contemplate going outside without many layers of clothes. Even though the temperature was often generous enough to rise above freezing, the ceaseless wind negated that gift, terrorising those who hadn't fattened up on the beef and king crab on sale in the local restaurants (one of which, not surprisingly, proclaimed itself to be 'The restaurant at the end of the world!').

•

Although Ushuaia has a pleasant local national park and a much-touted glacier (even if it turned out to be little bigger than an ice cube), and in spite of the fact that I'd got to see several species of bird new to me, and watched a single and illegal boat flare (illegal because of the wind— any fireworks could set the town alight) usher in a new year and decade, it just wasn't life-changing in the way I'd hoped my first stop in Patagonia would be. Unfortunately, just as I came to this realisation I found out there were no available seats on buses out of the place for over a week, so the only way I could depart was by plane once again.

The flight out of Ushuaia was as beautiful and exciting as the one in, mountains clutching at the plane's wingtips as it climbed, climbed, climbed above the snow, before dipping almost immediately.

I was on my way to the small town of El Calafate, still in Patagonia but further north, and not as obsessed with its location as Ushuaia is. There, I hoped, I would find the wildness, find everything that made Patagonia famous. Luckily I had no idea of the disaster I was setting myself up for.

The Empanada Disaster

Riding the bus from the airport into El Calafate, I felt a tingle of excitement as I took in the scenery, which was bare but not in that manufactured, blasted way humans so often create. Instead its barrenness was that of a landscape no machine could modify. After the streets of Ushuaia, with all those trinkets that were as authentic and tacky as a porn star's moans, this felt special. It felt wild.

My attention drawn by a sudden movement on the plain I recognised a guanaco, a wild relative of the llama. Beaming as I do whenever I see an animal for the first time (and often on subsequent viewings too), I turned to my fellow passengers to see if anyone else shared my delight, but saw nothing but bland disinterest on their faces. When the next animal I spotted turned out to be a rhea, a large flightless bird that was also new to me, I kept my face pressed to the glass and enjoyed the sight by myself, not losing my grin even when we hit a bump in the road and my head bounced away from and then violently back into the window.

The landscape changed several times on our way into town, each change thrillingly different from the previous scene—the plain yielding to clefted red rocks, then to rounded hills, then to views of distant forested mountains. This was the place, I was sure. This was the place I would find the real wild Patagonia.

The central part of El Calafate turned out to be touristy, with buildings made of timber so rough-hewn it must have been aimed at creating a sort of rustic charm, but triple varnished so it gleamed like no wood should. The price of food was so high it was also clearly aimed at tourists. Still, you only had to venture down a side street to find the places where the locals ate, identifiable as such because they were crowded and because no one inside them was wearing branded outdoor gear.

The best food in most places is rarely found in tourist joints because restaurateurs in those places don't have to worry about tourists coming back, only about getting them in the door. But if you cater to locals, your food needs to be good. And cheap. If the customers of a café or restaurant all went quiet when I entered, like the moment in a Western before a gunfight erupts, I knew I must be in the right place. Even if baleful glares and unresponsive service staff showed I wasn't particularly welcome, the food was bound to be worth it.

Using this theory, I found an empanada restaurant which literally sold only empanadas, a sort of pie stuffed with fish, meat or vegetables. No pizzas, no burgers, no appeal-to-the-tourists llama steaks, just empanadas. If you wanted a soft drink, you had to cross the road to the general store. I ordered six of the little pasties, and ate them for lunch as I made my way to a lagoon I'd seen on a map of the region, cutting through back streets instead of taking the regular paved route. It was a mistake, but an enlightening one.

Dust puffed from my heels, swirling up and away on the violent wind which also caught the omnipresent plastic bags and pinned them to bushes and trees. Empty bottles swept by, glass ones tinkling, plastic ones drumming, while turkey vultures overhead simultaneously battled the gale and tried to determine what in the scene below them was dead and what was garbage. The amount of litter was staggering, and made the neat streets I had just come from seem like deliberate fakery by the town fathers, like an apparently pristine apple that is rotten from the skin back.

Naturally, garbage had no respect for the fence that marked the perimeter of the small reserve where the lagoon was located, so scattered in the water among the ducks, coots, flamingos and geese were pink, blue and green shopping bags. Though I was excited to see birds in the lagoon I had never seen before, I worried for them, feeding amid such a lethal buffet.

As I walked around to the far side of the lagoon I felt my stomach flop, then flip, then twist, then gurgle and splutter. I clutched it in sudden pain, all the while trying to focus on whether it really was a Chiloe wigeon I was looking at.

As my hands started to shake I told myself that it would pass, sure that as with so many other lurgies I'd had in both Africa and South America this would be a small thing, and that the best course of action was to ignore it and carry on. So carry on I did, wandering around the reserve watching birds, saying hello to some horses that lived there, patting the stray dogs who followed me everywhere as if I were some sort of canine messiah (which would have been quite flattering if I'd had no sense of smell and couldn't detect their malodour). Finally, I headed back to the hostel along litter-laden streets, battling against the wind. Sinister gurgles were emanating from my mid-section by the time I reached the hostel, but I hoped they might diminish if I lay down for a while.

They did not, staying with me through a dinner that I could only pick at. I forced myself to eat something because I figured I'd need my strength for the next day, when I planned on hiking on the Perito Moreno glacier; indeed, I was already in possession of a pricey ticket to do just that.

I was staying in a share room, and had been allocated a top bunk over a sizable Italian woman with the most extraordinarily frizzy grey hair—it looked like a pompom that had been thrown into the wash with a Goth's clothing. I felt sorry for her having to put up with me tossing, turning and tossing some more, trying to find some relief for my painful stomach. For the first time in years I felt genuinely lonely and homesick, but not for any place that I could name.

As the night wore on, the pain worsened, until it felt as if I was being jabbed by spears. Out of consideration for the other occupants of the room I went into the hallway, checking the time as I went. It was two am and I had to be up in mere hours for the hike. Finally abandoning my pointless stoicism I approached the front desk where—against time-honoured international tradition—the night watchman was actually awake.

'Hello,' he said with a genuinely warm smile.

'Hello,' I replied, trying to return his smile but grimacing as I experienced another spasm. 'I think I need a doctor,' I managed through gritted teeth.

'Oh no, what's wrong?' he said, frowning sympathetically.

'I . . .' was all I could manage before—for the first time in my life—I collapsed to the floor in pain.

I was vaguely aware of the night watchman helping me up from where I lay gasping on the ground, putting me in a chair, and calling a cab to take me to the local hospital.

'I finish in three hours,' he said, after introducing himself as Julio. 'If you aren't back by then I'll come and find you.'

At his kindness I didn't feel lonely anymore; I wanted to express my gratitude but fell to the ground again as I was being poured into the taxi, banging my easily injured knee against the sill. I lay face down against the cracked vinyl for the short trip to the hospital; once there I half limped, half staggered towards the emergency room, where a nurse seemed startled to see me.

Glancing in a mirror above the reception desk I saw an unfamiliar face. It was pale, drawn, and looked fifty-five, not thirty-five. Even more dire, it was topped by a mullet haircut. Accidentally growing a mullet has been a sad but regular occurrence in my life ever since the hair on top of my head stopped growing as fast as the hair at the back. At least I was in the right country for such a travesty this time, as Argentinian men often have coifs not even an eighties rock band would have contemplated.

A doctor soon came to examine me and with no common language we used a mixture of pantomime and, on my part, the imbecile's way of speaking Spanish, which is to talk in English with an 'o' tacked onto the end of words. This combination sometimes works, and many symptoms were covered in this manner before the doctor asked if I was suffering from diarrhoea, which, though far more sensibly spelled in Spanish (*diarrea*), is pronounced the same way as in English.

'No,' I replied in all honesty.

My answer was met with a cocked eyebrow suggesting disbelief. '*Seguro?*' he asked. 'Are you sure?' A strange question, I thought. How could you *not* know?

I answered that I was sure, and he asked me again, and this time I understood his concern. 'I'm not embarrassed!' I said, or at least tried to say, before recalling that *embarazada* means something entirely different to 'embarrassed' and that I'd just wailed at the doctor that I wasn't pregnant, something his medical training had presumably made evident to him.

With this hurdle cleared (by now I *was* embarrassed) and having explained that any bulge in my stomach was made of empanadas, not a baby, we covered other symptoms. My limp was from banging my knee (that took some pantomime; and I decided against indicating that the scarring was caused by a puma), and I had no pain elsewhere apart from my stomach. I couldn't believe that an empanada (or several) had managed to do what Roy could not, and put me in hospital.

The doctor left the room with a frown and my homesickness suddenly returned. My funds were low, cheap food was all I could afford, yet my gut was mad as hell about my eating whatever low-priced fare was placed in front of me. Perhaps Patagonia was trying to kill me for failing to appreciate its charms. Was Friederike right—was I asking too much of this place, wanting something exclusive that in reality I couldn't afford? Or had I been wrong when I experienced my Jane Goodall epiphany, and perhaps I was too old and pathetic for my body to withstand the assaults it had shrugged off in my twenties?

The doctor returned with a needle that would have frightened a rhino, and a painkilling tablet the size of a small loaf of bread. With little ceremony he jabbed the needle into my backside. Miraculously, within minutes the writhing subsided, and soon I was feeling fine; in fact I felt so good by the time I made my way back through the hostel doors that morning that I *was* a little embarrassed. Anything that simple to cure shouldn't have needed a doctor, I felt, blushing as I thanked Julio.

'*De nada*,' he said. 'It's nothing.'

I returned to the dorm room as the first light seeped through the curtains, disturbingly illuminating just how skimpy some Italian underwear is, and managed to sleep for an hour before the alarm beeped rudely in my ear, waking me for the Perito Moreno hike.

In that state of near drunkenness that exhaustion can induce, I could scarcely recall the agony of the night before. I was excited. Finally I was going to see something special, I was sure of it.

And just for once, I was right.

•

I watched in wonder as a minivan-sized piece of ice dropped from the sheer face of the Perito Moreno glacier in front of us. 'That was huge!' I exclaimed, my voice hoarse from lack of sleep.

'Not so big,' one of the guides said nonchalantly.

We were on a boat that would take us to the base of the glacier, the sight of which had already stunned me into rare silence until the enormous block of ice fell away.

Moments later we were docking, and a group of us then began walking on a trail through light forest. Sheer cliffs launched skywards to our left, with waterfalls that regularly sprayed us as we walked. I tilted my head to catch some moisture on my tongue and almost toppled backwards.

A condor soared from over the ridgeline; even though it was hundreds of feet overhead its almost three-metre wingspan was staggering. 'Wow,' I said, my wildlife-spotting grin already in place.

This was what I'd been searching for when I came to Patagonia, but hadn't found in either El Calafate or Ushuaia. Patagonia had inspired writers, artists, naturalists and soul-searchers for hundreds of years; its remoteness had attracted the mad, the adventurous and the hunted. I felt sane enough, and while I was fleeing the mundane, as far as I knew I wasn't being chased. All I sought was the wildness and isolation that I'd missed so much living a 'normal' life in Sydney.

Still grinning, and lagging a little behind the others, I brushed my hands against lichen-heavy tree trunks, savouring the sensation of soft mosses underfoot. I caught up to the rest of the group at a staging point where the guides were putting them into uncomfortable-looking harnesses that bulged in unflattering places, making all of us, even the women, look like we'd sprung a grand tumescence at the activity planned.

I was soon rigged up and then the guide handed me what looked like a grand inquisitor's roller skates. I've always thought 'crampon' is one of the language's least attractive words, sounding like the bastard hybrid between something that causes pain and an item men are mortified to buy on behalf of their wives. But crampons on our boots would be essential here, their jagged metal teeth giving much-needed traction on the ice.

Clumsy at the best of times, I teetered as I hesitantly stepped onto the ice from the gravelly surface where we'd geared up, immediately forgetting any concerns of balance or verticality as I soaked up the view in front of me. The glacier was inconceivably vast. On my right it stretched back down to the lake from which we'd come. To the left it was a daunting, chunky, corrugated mass of blue and white for miles until it disappeared into mist, from the top of which poked snow-capped Andean peaks. This was totally unlike the jungly, fetid South America of my imagination, and the surprise thrilled me.

If I'd done more research I might have had the foresight to pack some warmer clothes. I had thought that the light sweater I'd put on after my brief sleep would be adequate, but most of the group were wearing coats so thick and shaggy you'd think they'd skinned Chewbacca's family.

'What makes the ice so blue?' an American woman in the group asked the guide. On our walk to the glacier this particular woman had delayed us twice by getting lost in an area only twice the size of a shoebox, and the group's collective patience with her was wearing a little thin.

'Smurf piss,' I answered; though I was joking the colour of the ice was so vivid it seemed as if it could only be fake. I'd never seen such an intensity of blue outside of a butterfly's wing, but unlike the flash of blue from a tropical moth in a forest, this went on for miles.

The woman looked at me blankly for a long moment.

'The ice crystals are packed so densely that the only light that reflects off it is in the blue spectrum,' our guide replied.

When I was a guide I might have run with the Smurf-urine theory just to see how long people believed me, but this guy was apparently more professional than I had ever been.

'Here's something,' said another guide, a New Zealander, as he hunched over a small dark object on the ice.

I clomped over, the crampon blades crunching into the ice with each step, and looked down to where he was pointing. Incongruous in this pristine environment, a turd sat starkly on the ice.

'Well hello, Roy,' I said. 'You following me?'

'You name your poo Roy?' the guide asked.

'Um, no, that's puma poo, and I had a puma named Roy.'

That undoubtedly made as much sense as my previous statement so I shut up. In Africa I used to hear stories of leopards turning up in unexpected places (a sports stadium in Cape Town, the summit of Kilimanjaro, and on a small island in the middle of the vast Lake Kariba). The leopards' adaptability and ability to survive in any habitat were legendary. While the jaguars I yearned to see might look more like leopards, I was learning that pumas were the continent's real equivalent.

As we went deeper into the glacier I concentrated on lifting my feet cleanly with each stride rather than shuffling lazily. If I put the spikes down on uneven ground or they caught because I dragged my feet I could be felled like a tree, hitting the hard blue ice face first. A slip and slide away from the carefully chosen route the guides were taking us on could lead to any number of deadly chasms. The guides pointed out one of these, and the sheer scale of the glacier became shockingly apparent as I peered down a shaft of over thirty metres, at the base of which water rushed as if possessed of a ferocious hunger.

My fear of heights kicked in and I was glad of the firm hold the New Zealand guide took on my belt. 'Easy, mate,' he said casually, and I realised I'd been swaying as I looked down into the chasm. With enormous concentration I lifted my clawed feet one by one and backed away from the hole.

We ate lunch soon after, some of us sitting on cloths that soon grew damp as the ice melted through them. Those who had brought plastic sheets probably felt smug—until their body heat melted a slick layer underneath the plastic, causing them to toboggan forward into the nearest obstacle (usually someone sitting on a cloth).

After lunch we were allowed to wander on the glacier by ourselves. I split from the others and made my way over mounds of ice carved into sensual shapes by wind and water, walking until I was out of sight of the group, then pausing, watching the steam of my breath plume in front of me in short bursts. It had taken Roy four weeks to get me fit and slim me down to wiry, and I'd spent the six weeks since piling weight back on at such a rate I was now fatter and less fit than when I'd first come to South America. After Roy I had the dedication to exercise of a sloth, and was rapidly getting the physique to match. I'd begun to find myself out of breath at the mere thought of doing something strenuous. Like chewing. I probably needed to do something about my weight, I thought, then stopped myself with a mental slap. I was trying to leave such city thoughts behind, avoiding places where what you looked like was important. In the wild, experience and ability are all that matter.

I stopped worrying about my gut and took in my surrounds. Around me was nothing but blue and white patterned ice, and I thought, 'If I was left behind here, I would surely die.' It had been years since I'd had such a thought, the last time being in the very different landscape of the deserts of Namibia. It was exhilarating to be able to think it again. In places where man is not dominant, but dwarfed and made insignificant by nature, I get an adrenalin rush. My time with Roy had been a rollercoaster-ride of adrenalin, but this was different. It was what I'd been missing for seven years. I promised myself to never again go without it for such a long time.

The feelings I had on the glacier have no name in English that I am aware of. It was a blend of respect for a place so inhospitable to my existence, coupled with gratitude that thus far it had not snuffed me out. Awe was also in there, as was a sort of love, both words so overused that they've lost much of their power. Contentment, that underrated emotion, was also present, but not for any good reason

I could think of. (What sort of person mellows out on a chunk of ice destined, albeit slowly, to go off a cliff?) All I knew was that right then if I'd had a tail I'd have wagged it.

Funnily enough, I hadn't expected to feel like this here, having previously only felt it in places where animals might eat me, and—snobbishly, naively—I hadn't expected to experience it on a group tour. I realised my guides would probably scoff at such feelings, just as I had once scoffed when people on my safari tours told me that they'd been sure they would die after receiving an aggressive look from some lion/elephant/sparrow. Maybe I owed a few people some apologies.

My reverie was interrupted by one of the guides, come to check that I hadn't fallen into a ravine. 'You okay?' he asked.

'Better than okay!' I shouted back.

Then it hit me: I'd just been soul searching. 'Well, I'll be,' I thought, surprised at myself. 'The place works!'

The Road from Patagonia

After the awe-inspiring magnificence of the Perito Moreno glacier I was brought back to earth with a thud by my next Patagonian stopover in a place called El Chaltén, a day's bus ride from El Calafate. My stay there turned out to be pleasant but unexciting; the rare and endangered deer species I had hoped to see turned out to be as elusive as a park ranger had predicted, and the pumas he'd told me other tourists had seen also stayed away. Even the well-known peak of Mt Fitz Roy stayed shrouded in fog.

El Chaltén's bars were filled with glum-looking climbers, some of whom had been waiting weeks for the notoriously temperamental weather to clear enough for them to summit. I was amazed that any cloud could stay put, as the wind was even fiercer than the other places I had been in Patagonia so far. It shoved me around like a schoolyard bully, making me wonder if maybe I should join the climbers for a few beers and fatten up even more.

As it turned out I might have been able to keep a better eye on my backpack in the bar: I returned from a trail walk to find my wallet emptied (I hadn't taken it with me due to stories of banditry on the paths, which in hindsight was ludicrous as the trails were too busy for a mugger to choose a target). El Chaltén's only cash machine was as empty as my wallet, and the nearest bank was in Bariloche, whose townspeople had figured out being considered part of Patagonia was a good thing, so had redrawn the region's boundary to include themselves. I wasn't sure that the small change in my pocket would be enough to buy food until I made it there, and was not looking forward to the trip. Little did I know how it would change my travels.

•

The crowd that formed for the bus to Bariloche was made up of a broad cross-section of humanity. All continents, ages, colours, shapes and heights were represented. Spotting an unusually tall blonde woman with pretty features, I wished (not for the first time) I had more confidence when it came to talking to attractive strangers.

Argentinian buses are remarkably punctual, and this one took off promptly at the time advertised. Within minutes we were chugging through spectacular mountain scenery, made all the more striking because the clouds had finally lifted. At each sharp turn in the road there was a small shrine, often in gaudy colours, marking the place where one or more vehicles had gone over the edge. These markers reflected a mix of Catholicism and the more ancient local traditions, with statues of Mary and Jesus as well as the brilliant colours and animal totems that harked back to a time before the Incas. As perturbing as the sheer number of these markers was, any anxiety was forgotten in the thrill of the falcon-haunted cliffs, multicoloured rock faces and distant snowy caps. (I resolutely faced these rather than looking at the terrifying drop off the other side of the road.)

I kept my face turned to the window, but happened to spot the tall blonde woman sitting a few rows back from me beside an even taller man. I envied him for a while until I noticed they weren't talking. 'They must be fighting,' I thought, and as a shorter man often will when a taller one suffers, felt a small pang of glee.

After a while, the engine noises changed from a hard-working grumble to a smoother purr. We had levelled out and abruptly left the mountains behind. The arid plain we emerged onto was so featureless that the world seemed nothing but horizon. Despite its silken-smooth appearance outside, the bullet-straight dirt track we were driving on was pitted and corrugated, making everyone's cheeks jiggle and teeth chatter.

I can find beauty in the stark, and I appreciated the view outside as much as any other. Occasionally the flat stretches were interrupted by a glimpse of a distant lake in shades of the most impossible deep blue or green. As the glaciers that fed these lakes ground away, they crushed rock into such a fine powder that when it reached the lakes it stayed suspended, and only allowed certain wavelengths of light to reflect, creating marvellous palettes. Just as colourful was the odd shrine, similar to those in the mountains but to my mind even more perturbing on a dead-flat road. The monotony was clearly soporific for some drivers and, judging by the slack drooling mouths of many around me, some passengers too. I started looking at the driver periodically to check whether the long straight road wasn't acting as a lullaby for him too.

Though I was happy taking in the view outside the window, some of the passengers who weren't sleeping wanted more stimulation, and to appease them the driver put on some videos. First was an American action film; the video had clearly been pirated and was dubbed into Russian, then translated back into English subtitles. Whoever had written the subtitles wasn't a native English speaker, or perhaps they had a juvenile sense of humour, for the word 'bomb' had been incorrectly translated, leading to not-quite-Shakespearean lines of dialogue such as: 'Oh no! He's got a bum!' and 'We don't know how big his bum is, but we do know it is powerful. It might take out a whole city.' At the film's midway point, translation duties must have been handed over to someone else, since one character's name suddenly and inexplicably changed from Gordon to Norman and all the unintentional bum jokes stopped.

The action film over, music videos began with a much more local flavour. Reggaeton originated in the Caribbean but spread quickly throughout South America. It has a jangly beat and is invariably accompanied by a clip of a man in large dark glasses surrounded by impressively proportioned dancers. The men snarl and rap, making hand gestures that I presume are meant to look like they're holding guns but make them appear palsied instead. After five hours of the music I was afraid my ears might vomit, but no relief was in sight.

While the videos alternated between bad and worse, the view outside retained my interest (with an occasional glance in the window's reflection to check on relations between the tall blonde and the man beside her; to my satisfaction, it didn't appear to have thawed). We stopped every few hours to stretch our legs and once for lunch. The bedraggled store we visited had a gutterless roof weighed down with stones, suggesting a place of howling winds but little rain. The soil was clearly poor, and it seemed all that grew here was despair. A sad-looking lamb near the store bleated at us plaintively, then went and sat beside an outdoor barbecue, as if aware of its eventual fate and more than ready to accept it.

The wind soon drove everyone back into the bus, and we hit the plain again, leaving the hapless store and suicidal lamb behind. At times the only feature outside at all was the bus's shadow, expanding and contracting as we rocked from side to side.

As night fell we reached a one-taxi town with the same name as the glacier I had fallen in love with, Perito Moreno. This place had far less charm though, consisting of a few stores selling auto parts and gasoline, and a single hotel run by a bear of a man and his three tiny daughters, all under ten, all working behind the bar. The cost of the bus ticket included accommodation, and I was billeted to a room, arriving at the same time as a slightly built German man who smiled heartily at me. Though clearly from a place where dentistry wasn't in vogue, he was very friendly and spoke perfect English. We spent at least five minutes insisting the other person should have the larger of the three beds in the room before agreeing to take the smaller ones and leave the bigger for whoever else was sharing with us.

The door opened and in walked the tall woman's even taller boyfriend.

'Where's your girlfriend?' the German and I asked almost simultaneously in Spanish, and I wondered if he of the bad dentistry had also shared rooms before with couples whose sense of discretion was no match for their randiness.

'I don't have a girlfriend,' the newcomer replied, looking at us as if wondering why he had to share a room with two deranged midgets.

We quickly established that he was French, that our only common language was a smattering of Spanish, and that the woman he'd been sitting next to on the bus was unknown to him, and that they'd hardly exchanged a word all day. He didn't know her name nor where she was from.

Interesting, I mused.

•

At six the next morning our three alarms rang, and six weary fists rubbed sleep from six eyes before we all politely argued over who should use the bathroom first. The Frenchman's bladder won.

Soon we were outside waiting for the bus, then were told to wait some more. And some more, a wait of more than three hours, before our original bus was declared dead and we were herded onto two replacement buses that must have been there all along. I landed on the second, only to watch the first bus peel away before hearing ours splutter and fart, then gurgle so wretchedly it was clearly the sound of something breathing its last.

'The bus is not fixed,' said our driver, which I thought was quite a clever spin on the situation.

Herded back off the bus we waited and watched the driver and a local mechanic's legs for half an hour. They moved little from their position jutting out from under the bus until a voice shouted 'Bravo!' and they emerged with greasy triumphant grins.

We clambered back on and for the first time I noticed that the tall blonde woman was on the same bus, in the seat immediately behind mine. I mustn't have rubbed the sleep out of my eyes hard enough.

'Bloody hell, if we don't move soon we'll never get there,' said an Australian accent behind me. It wasn't the tall woman (who I'd begun to think of as 'the good-looking tall woman *without* a French boyfriend'), but the woman in the seat next to her.

Never one to miss an opportunity, I swapped names with the Australian (hers was Ange) and we soon figured out we were both from Sydney. The blonde looked out the window, occasionally flicking her eyes towards Ange and me as we chatted. I presumed she was from somewhere Nordic and was bound to have that enviable

European ability of casually speaking half a dozen languages. (If you ever express admiration for their learning they seem astonished. 'You don't?' is the implication in their reply.)

Back to taking in the view outside, at one point I shouted 'Armadillo!', startling those around me, except the now frustratingly impassive tall blonde sans French boyfriend, who continued staring out the window. The animal I had seen had dashed away from our looming tyres and dived into a culvert, so I was left in the awkward position of explaining that I had indeed seen an armadillo, but that it was now gone. I glanced at the blonde, wondering why she was so aloof, then saw the telltale trail of headphone cords in her hair.

Doofus! I said to myself. Still, I had to admire her method of blocking out the reggaeton.

In any case, we didn't get far before the bus began a series of hopping lurches. The driver managed to coax it on a few more kilometres to a service station, where we were instructed simply to get off the bus and 'wait'.

It could have been frustrating, but years in Africa had taught me that impatience only gives you wrinkles, so it's best to make the most of such situations. At least we were liberated from the confines of bus seats that were as wide as toothpicks and about as comfortable to put your buttocks on.

Still intrigued by the tall blonde I sidled closer to her, keen to impress but with little to offer in the way of witty banter. I decided instead to stick to the one subject I can talk confidently about, and fortunately and animal soon approached. I watched it a moment until it began behaviour I recognised, which I interpreted for her benefit: 'Oh look! That cat's about to puke!'

'Um, thanks for showing me that,' she said, blinking in disbelief.

'You're English?' I asked, startled not to hear a Nordic lilt.

'Welsh actually,' she said.

I mentally kicked myself. I should have spotted the difference.

'But both my parents are English,' she added, 'so my accent is a bit mixed up.'

This little piece of self-deprecation made my small but burgeoning crush crank up a notch. It ratcheted up further as our conversation continued and she mentioned she was a fan of rugby. 'And Wales is the best team in the world,' she announced.

'Ranked about sixth officially though, aren't they?' I said.

The withering look she gave me made it clear I'd blundered again. It had been some years since I'd simultaneously been single and spoken with an attractive woman. I was clearly still not good at it.

I really wanted whatever I said next to be at least correct, if not impressive, so I thrust out my hand as if in a business meeting and said, 'My name's Peter.'

'Lisa,' she replied, shaking my hand with a slight smirk, presumably at my awkwardness.

'Nice name,' I said, then felt foolish. 'But I think I will call you the Minke,' I added impulsively.

I couldn't believe it. Had I just nicknamed her after a *whale*? What self-destructive urge had taken over my tongue?

'Why?' she asked.

At this point a smarter person would have backtracked, issued a blanket denial or pleaded a brain injury. I said, weakly, 'Because you're from Wales.' Apparently unable to stop myself, I continued, 'And because you're big.'

I gulped, tasting the feet I had just placed firmly in my mouth.

Unbelievably, the Minke smiled. 'That's pretty odd,' she said, 'but I like it!'

'Wow,' I thought, genuinely impressed. I hadn't meant the name as an insult (to me no animal name is an insult) but most women would not be so gracious about being compared to an animal weighing several tonnes. At least I hadn't called her Humpback. My little crush grew like a plankton bloom, and I resolved to be cool and not make any more references to sea creatures.

So it was that I spent the next hour hanging around the Minke, and when we were finally allowed back on the bus I soon developed a neck strain from constantly turning around to talk to her.

The neck injury grew worse when, with a squeal of brakes and a spray of gravel, the bus came to a juddering halt. Our driver leapt from the vehicle as if it were in flames, and ran onto the gravel area at the side of the bus. Something scuttled ahead of him, jinking as he jagged, but with nowhere to hide in the featureless landscape.

'Armadillo!' I shouted again, delighted to see another one, though I immediately became concerned about how it would be treated. The armadillo's frantic movement finally ceased as the driver pinned the animal with his foot, which probably wasn't as uncomfortable as it looked given all the armour armadillos carry. Armadillos are the only animal apart from humans susceptible to leprosy, and I thought about telling the driver this so he would let it go, but lacked the Spanish words to say, 'Keep touching that and parts may well begin to drop off you.'

I got off the bus with a few others, including the Minke, to get a better look, the omnipresent wind sandblasting skin already tender from weeks of rough weather. I looked at the little creature being pinned to the ground and wondered how far I would go to set it free.

To my relief, the driver did not take the animal for the cooking pot but let it go, and it scooted off into the eternal horizon, puffs of dust spurting from its tiny feet as it went. We all got back on the bus, and the Minke told me she was delighted to have seen it. 'Armadillo!' she said. 'Crunchy on the outside, soft on the inside!' Seeing my hesitant grin she added, 'You don't get the reference, do you?'

I shook my head.

'Why don't you explain it over dinner if we all go out tomorrow?' suggested Ange (now a fully fledged Angel in my mind) and I could have kissed her but felt it might send a mixed signal.

•

Some hours later there was a dramatic shift in scenery, and after a small dip in the road that didn't seem to signify anything of great note, pine trees appeared outside, along with many other forms of vegetation I'd never seen before. The light through the windows waned; soon after, clusters of lights in the distance announced our arrival on the outskirts of Bariloche.

For some reason a pensive mood overtook me after leaving the bus. Patagonia had not been what I'd expected. Admittedly I'd only seen a small patch of it but it had only been on the glacier that I'd felt the sense of isolation for which Patagonia was famous. Somehow, the armadillo incident seemed to sum up the Patagonia I'd seen—once wild, but now held down and subdued. Instead of experiencing an untamed Patagonia, I had been yet another pair of human feet domesticating it.

I pondered this while gazing absentmindedly at an Argentinian woman with a flushed-faced baby waiting for a bus that would take her back in the direction we had just come. There was something odd about the baby that I couldn't quite put my finger on. Then I realised that its cheeks were not merely ruddy, but blotched, blasted and burned, not by sun but by the abrasive air. I sympathised with it, already feeling a cold sore developing that would eventually take the shape of Italy, and become almost the same size.

Then it hit me. They might build roads in Patagonia, they might catch every armadillo and put a trinket store on every corner. But the place could never be tamed while that wind blew, and that thought, as well as my impending date with Lisa, made my cracked lips spread into a painful smile.

The Joy of Pessimism

Over steaks and malbec (Argentina's signature wine), Lisa and I discovered that our travel plans overlapped in many places, and we decided to tackle South America together for a while. Ange chaperoned us for one night only before her short trip ended, leaving the Minke and me to continue on the road as a twosome. After two more nights in Bariloche we would start making our way by bus yet again (the Andes are a dramatic addition to South America's scenery, but have precluded much of the continent from developing railways). We began a meandering journey into Bolivia, and took the unappealingly named Death Train (so called allegedly because for every passenger inside there used to be one surfing the roof, and many fell off as fatigue or alcohol loosened their grip) to the Brazilian border.

'Do you really not mind me calling you the Minke?' I asked one day, fearful that she might just be tolerating it out of politeness.

'No, I really do like it! But you can use my name at times if you can remember it.'

'Of course I do.' I paused, as if dredging my memory. 'Ailsa? No, that's not it. Alisa? No, close, I'm sure . . .' and she gave me a playful wallop; while I was thrilled at the contact I was also startled by her reach. If we did get together, as I hoped, I was very glad that I was a runner, not a fighter.

We made our way across Bolivia and into Brazil, arriving at the town of Miranda, and there we met a guide who had been recommended to me, a burly man with the strong, angular features of the region's indigenous people, the Kadiweu people. His name was Marcello, and he was passionate about the very animal I so wanted to see.

Soon after meeting Marcello I decided I liked him, for a strange reason. We were travelling towards the Pantanal, a famous wetland often compared to my beloved Okavango Delta in Botswana, a haven for wildlife of all sorts. We'd gone there to see the astonishing birds it was known for, as well as capybaras (the world's largest rodent, a guinea pig that weighs more than a supermodel), alligators and tapirs, an animal that is pig-shaped and elephant-snouted but is in fact most closely related to rhinos and horses. The Pantanal is also famous for jaguars.

As well as being extremely knowledgeable about the Pantanal, Marcello also had an affinity for the big cat I sought. He was intrigued by my background as a guide, and as we drove from Miranda into the wetlands we swapped stories of lunatic tourists before reverting to the topic we both loved most—animals. I briefly wondered whether he might be putting on a passion he didn't really feel as part of his customer service.

The road we were on was tarred, and the few cars we encountered were travelling fast. Cane grew high on either side of the road; suddenly a scraggly-looking chicken stepped out from the tight clusters of cane and decided to cross the road, intent, it seemed, on suicide. By sheer chance, at that exact moment a car appeared, coming towards us, which meant that to swerve around the chicken would result in a head-on collision. So Marcello held his course, and there was a loud *dong* from under the vehicle.

'I'm so sorry,' Marcello said. 'So sorry,' he repeated, and I could see his brown knuckles go a shade paler from gripping the wheel so tightly. Maybe he wasn't apologising to the chicken, maybe it was to the Minke and me, but I could see a real tear in his eye. This was exactly the sort of guide I wanted.

Marcello knew my aim—to see a jaguar in the wild, along the way picking up as many other feathered and furred species as I could.

'It is not the right season for jaguars,' he said, 'but you never know.'

I'd said exactly the same thing over the years to tourists who hoped to see some elusive bird or animal, and as much of a platitude as it sounds, it's true: you never do know. Jaguars tend not to migrate, but in the drier season they have more open land to roam in, and are thus harder to find. For some reason, though, I was feeling lucky, and was sure that we would see a jaguar in our few days with Marcello.

While we were in Miranda, the Minke and I had met Marcello's wife, Miranda, plus his three dogs, including a puppy he'd rescued from a caiman (a type of alligator). The puppy's mother had been poisoned by some hard-hearted individual, and she had died beside the lagoon edge. A caiman had appreciated the easy meal, and had also taken several of her mourning puppies before Marcello grabbed the sole survivor. The Minke had become enamoured with the puppy as soon as she met him, and I think she was just as happy seeing him as any jaguar. But before we even tried to meet a jaguar, almost impossible in the heat of the day, we would meet the caiman.

'It's huge!' Marcello said. 'Huge!' he reiterated. 'At least eight feet!'

Two and a half metres? I almost snorted in a way that would have revealed my wildlife snobbery. In both Australia and Africa, 'huge' means a crocodile is at least twice the size of a human. (There are records in both places of crocodiles over six metres long; the skeleton of a true dinosaur estimated to have been ten metres was once recorded in Australia.) Two and a half metres is large enough to do damage, but I doubted such an animal could take you down. Still, our plan was to swim with it, and that made my armpits a little sticky.

'It was right there,' said Marcello, indicating the spot with a machete he kept holstered on his belt at all times (I wondered if he slept with it). 'Huge!' he said again, and I started to like him more, just for his enthusiasm.

The Minke and I changed into swimwear, Marcello just waded into the water in his black T-shirt and shorts, and soon we were in a lagoon beside a gently flowing stream. We paddled around, Marcello explaining that the caiman was curious and would often bob to the surface, and slowly approach, coming as close as a foot away. There were also piranhas in the water, but I was less nervous about them. I had read that despite their mythic voraciousness for meat, most piranhas are primarily vegetarian but will scavenge on occasion, and only if trapped in a shrinking pool turn into savage flesh-tearing monsters.

We paddled around, and I even went into the deeper water, but the caiman didn't show and it occurred to me that if it had recently eaten a poisoned dog it could well not be in the best of health. Then again, reptile digestive systems can handle almost anything.

As we came out of the water Marcello pointed to a tree down the road, and we approached it. The tree had four vertical scratches carved deep into the bark. This was territorial marking by a big cat, something I was used to from the jaguar's African cousins. But these were widely spaced, and high up. The animal that had made these *was* huge.

'Huge!' Marcello said, echoing my thoughts.

We drove on from the swimming spot, and I noted with some regret just how many roads there were in the area. To build these roads, areas of wetland needed to be disturbed, which was in itself bad enough for the environment; but while the roads made travelling easy for tourists such as us, it also made access to the region easier for people with ill intent. This was brought starkly home when Marcello stopped the car and we walked towards some vultures we had seen circling, then dropping, at a point not far from the road. It turned out the target of the vultures' interest was a caiman, this one no threat to us because of a bullet hole in its head and a hacked-off tail.

'Poachers,' Marcello said. 'They will sell the meat to restaurants.'

We stood in respectful silence, like mourners at a funeral; there was no need to voice our disgust.

'Shame,' said Marcello, breaking the silence. 'He was huge.'

We drove back to the camp where we were staying, showered, and prepared for an afternoon boat ride: the river was one of the finest vantage points for jaguar spotting since they often sun themselves on the banks. I felt a tingle of anticipation about our expedition.

As we set out the atmosphere was electric, and so were the eels. One briefly swam to the surface, and despite a lunatic compulsion to grab it to see just how strong the shock would be, I resisted. I had read that they could produce a high enough voltage to stop your heart. 'People here fear these eels more than piranhas,' Marcello explained. 'It is only your movies that make people think piranhas are bad.' No more swimming in this part of the river. Time to find a jaguar.

I tried to repress the enthusiasm I was feeling, something I do often. For years I've believed that pessimists are the happiest people on earth because they're never disappointed, and frequently have more pleasant surprises than do starry-eyed optimists. Though I am occasionally accused of cynicism, none is needed to maintain low hopes. I also believe that the anticipation is often better than the reward (this works in reverse too—a needle hurts far less than the expectation of it).

That afternoon my bird-species count advanced at the pace of a child chasing an ice-cream truck—as we glimpsed Jabiru storks, scarlet ibis, wonderful Toco toucans with their absurd banana beaks, and Mardi Gras–coloured macaws. Unfortunately a jaguar failed to materialise.

That night we ate freshly caught fish from the river we'd just been on, and slurped thirstily at icy-cold beers before moving onto caipirinhas. This Brazilian specialty is delicious, sweet and sour: a cocktail so refreshing it's impossible to stop at one. We didn't, and were soon roaring with laughter at each other's stories. Marcello had a bounty of jaguar tales, and I countered with stories of elephants and lions. With some guides the swapping of stories can become competitive, but this was just easy banter, and the Minke laughed at all of them, even though by now she'd already heard most of my stories as I tried to impress her with decade-old adventures, never mentioning the dull intervening years.

I lost track of the rounds of drinks we consumed, and while we needed to be up early (as is the case for almost any wildlife-spotting endeavour), the stories just kept coming. Rather than the animals we'd observed, many of our stories focused more on the tourists we'd led and their follies, and how hard it could be at times not to poke your own eyes out in frustration at their antics.

At one point I found myself asking Marcello what it was he loved about guiding.

'I love the Pantanal,' he said, with a resigned shrug. 'I want others to love it too.'

I understood. I felt the same way about Africa's wild places. But the next thing he described was something I had never experienced.

'I was born here, a real Indian, in a tribe that lived in those hills that I showed you. I don't even know how old I am, because we had no watches or calendars. We just hunted, fished, and lived with the animals, like animals.'

I was initially surprised to hear him say they lived like animals, but then I thought that maybe it was only in Western culture that the comparison would be considered derogatory. Such a strong link to a place as Marcello felt to the Pantanal was something that as a nomad I could not comprehend. For a moment I envied Marcello his deep roots, but that was only because I hadn't yet heard the rest of his story.

'Sometimes we would meet outsiders, but mostly we tried to avoid them. All they wanted was to take,' he said, then hesitated. 'Then some diamond miners came, and wanted what was under our land.' He paused again, longer this time, and took a long draught from his drink. I signalled the barman, who began crushing limes for another round.

'My people didn't want the mine, so the miners attacked us,' Marcello continued, and now the Minke and I realised this was a very different story from those we had heard so far. 'They tied us up, and then attacked my mother. My father got free, and ran to help her, so they shot him. Then they shot my mother.' Marcello's face was red and crumpled with anguish, and a tear made its way along the creases.

'I ran away, and kept running,' he said. 'I never went back. Some days later, I was found on a farm by some people who took me in. It was in the papers, that an Indian had been found on a farm, but I couldn't tell anyone what had happened because nobody spoke my language.

'I worked on the farm of the people who found me, and they adopted me, teaching me Portuguese. Then one day a neighbour had some tourists on his farm. He had heard that I was good at finding animals, so I helped with the tourists, and that is how I started guiding, learning English and some German too.'

'You were very lucky that those people found you and took you in,' the Minke said.

Marcello shrugged. 'Yes . . . but they used to beat me. So much.'

The Minke and I both rocked back in our chairs, appalled.

Marcello's broad shoulders shook with some suppressed memory. 'I want a daughter,' he said suddenly, changing the subject, 'because they don't get distracted like men do, chasing money and women, and she will learn languages so she can speak to everyone, and I will teach her to be the best guide in the Pantanal and show all these idiots guiding how to do it. They don't love the Pantanal, they just want the tips. I want a daughter to do what I do. That would make a good future for this place.'

'You're an optimist,' I said, leaving it at that, but wanting to commend him for his strength after all the hardships he had faced.

'What else can you be?' he asked simply.

Later that night the Minke and I wended our way along the path back to our rooms. 'After that I really feel any complaints I have about my life are petty,' the Minke said.

'Me too,' I agreed, and could add no more. I felt chastened when I remembered all the times I'd thought my life was hard, and flattered that Marcello shared such an insight. I was driven to protect animals because they mattered to me, but Marcello had a sense of ownership, kinship even, that I could only grasp at. Perhaps I needed to learn from Marcello. His life had dealt him more than I could probably have coped with, and he still held hope, and desire to do good. Borrowing some of his optimism, as the Minke and I reached the doors to our separate rooms I overcame my shyness, took her hand and pulled her close. She was a full head taller than me, but felt light, like bird wings. Then I reached up, and kissed her.

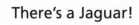

The next morning, foggy headed and with hyena breath from the caipirinhas, but not in such poor shape that we couldn't get up, the Minke and I met Marcello and a driver, and set out again by boat. This time we were joined by two Germans who might have wondered why I couldn't stop smiling.

We went well away from areas used by other tourists and casual fishermen. The Pantanal was again vibrant with birds, but mammals made an appearance as well—howler monkeys high in the treetops blended well with their surrounds, despite their shiny red fur, while capybaras lazed by the banks, looking remarkably content as the sun's first rays warmed them.

Eventually we stopped at an island formed by a myriad of intersecting channels, and set up there for the day. Marcello had seen a jaguar's tracks there a few days earlier, and felt that she might have come this way again. The two Germans were just as keen as I was to see a jaguar, so we eagerly set off on a trail, attempting to pick our path carefully but somehow managing to tread on every crackly leaf, every snapping twig, while Marcello's broad bare feet moved noiselessly over the forest floor.

I scanned the ground for tracks, seeing the hippo-like splayed-toe tracks of capybara; the pads and claw marks of some smaller predator that I couldn't identify, maybe a raccoon species; a fox's clear prints—

but no sign of a large cat. Marcello looked from side to side, up and down, as trackers do, but he also found nothing to indicate a jaguar had passed this way.

It was another bust, but the area was so idyllic that I couldn't feel too disappointed. The boatman had strung up hammocks while we walked, and we lazed in these under the shade of canopied trees while he cooked us a lunch of more fresh fish, the river flowing gently by mere metres away. After eating we returned to more lazing, and then I felt the need for some exercise, and decided to go for a swim.

I wandered upstream until I reached an open section of the bank, the muddy trail down to the water dense with capybara tracks. I waded in, feeling a current far stronger than the mellow surface had led me to believe. Lisa soon joined me, and in a sheltered, slow-flowing part of the river we splashed at each other, and I went to chase her. In a few long-limbed strokes she was so far ahead of me that pursuit was clearly futile. Like most Australians I am confident in the water, but the ease with which she outswam me stripped away some of my assurance and put a small dent in my ego. I recalled her once saying she'd represented Wales in swimming, so I shouldn't have been surprised, nor as concerned when she swam straight into the strongest part of the current and disappeared around a curve in the river.

'Minke?' I called after her. 'You okay?'

'Fine,' she said casually, stroking easily back into view, a feat that would leave me panting and close to cardiac arrest if I tried it. Then she let the current take her again, and was lost to my sight once more.

But there was something else in the water with us. Close to the bank opposite me a dark head appeared, then another beside it. They were only ten metres from me but it took me some moments to

Above: Roy the puma loved his jungle trails, but also had a strange penchant for walking on top of pipes. The Roy Boys would try to emulate him—the first person to slip had to buy that evening's beers. And would most likely get bitten for their impudence.

Right: Pumas and jaguars may seem fierce, but South America's deadliest animals are frogs with skin so poisonous just touching them can be fatal. I probably shouldn't have picked this little fellow up then.

Below: This squirrel monkey made himself an inverted hammock outside my room at Sacha Lodge.

Cabbage Patch Kids grow up eventually. Maybe one day I will too.

Left: Detail of a Bird of Paradise flower, an example of the extravagant flora in the Amazon basin.

. . . almost as extravagant as the insect life (right)—this fellow is a Lantern or Peanut Bug. The Kichwa believe that if one bites you you must have sex within 24 hours or die. I'm pretty sure a man came up with that.

The amazing Omagewe, born before his tribe (the Huaorani) had any contact with the outside world and still living a mostly traditional lifestyle. He showed me the jungle in a way few living people could.

The caecilian looks like an overgrown earthworm the size of a snake, but is neither. It is one of the bizarre animals that attracted me to South America—an amphibian that lives underground.

Getting fitted for my string (made from the fibres of a local palm tree)—the string would be all I wore for much of my time with the Huaorani.

... all I wore apart from sunscreen, which I was sorely in need of, and merely sore without.

As my time with the Huaorani wore on, stocks from the outside world dwindled. This smoked chicken would be my last familiar meat and soon I was sampling paca (a long-legged forest relative of the guinea pig) among other new treats.

This fish and cassava would have been delicious on any other day, but a mystery lurgy laid me low and I almost offended my hosts by refusing it.

Omagewe's wife (whose name I could never pronounce) made this loom in less than a minute, then wove me armbands, which included strands of Omagewe's hair that he hacked from his head with a machete.

Many of the older Huaorani dress traditionally most days, despite having access to modern clothing.

I kept a diary for the first time in twenty years while in Yasuni National Park with the Huaorani, and kept it despite the moulding humidity and occasional interruptions, like this Borer beetle that fell from the thatch onto the page.

A Dwarf Caiman, innocuous as it never grows to more than two metres. I was very happy to see it, but more than anything I wanted to see a jaguar.

The longest blowdarts in the Amazon are made by the Huaorani, but are meant to shoot things above them, such as birds or monkeys, and are too heavy to hold straight in front of you as I am attempting here.

Otobo holds a lantern bug, maybe wondering if his wife will believe the Kichwa legend about them.

establish what I was seeing. Then two more heads appeared, and one looked directly at me, its sleek head swivelling on a submerged neck, dark brown eyes expressionless as they took me in.

'Giant otters!' I shouted gleefully, forgetting all the times I'd berated tourists for speaking loudly around animals. But the otters ignored me. The largest of the otter family (as the name suggests), giant otters can weigh up to thirty-five kilograms, and while they look cute they're known to be aggressively territorial and vicious in defence of their young.

Surely they wouldn't see *me* as any sort of threat, I thought, and did an inelegant flop into deeper water, immediately feeling the tug of the flow. My plan had been to swim across to the other side where the otters were holding almost still, backstroking into the current with no visible effort. But angling into the current soon sapped my energy, and before I could reach them the otters casually flicked their tails and took off downstream, their heads bobbing lightly as if they were laughing at my feebleness. With no hope of catching up to them, I turned to go back, only to see the bank where I had entered the water rapidly disappearing as the current took me. I swam towards it nevertheless, but below me was a mess of tangled vegetation and I was wary of snags that could trap an ankle and pull me under.

There was no going back to my entry point; all I could do was follow the otters and Lisa downstream and try to get out where the boat was. A fast-moving object stroked my belly; most likely it was only a branch swept by the current, but travelling at speed it could cut me deeply, and that would surely excite nearby piranhas. Feeling foolish, and wondering once again why I always felt so compelled to get close to animals, I made cautious backwards strokes to slow myself, but was still moving fast enough to hit our boat at ramming speed, generating a resonant *dong* from its hull.

'*Tutto bong?*' the boatman asked me as I clutched the side of the boat, trying desperately to look calm and unflustered while gasping like a dying goldfish.

'*Tutto bong,*' I replied, two of the only words I know in Portuguese, which mean 'all okay'.

'You just hit the boat, didn't you?' the Minke asked. She presumably had had far less difficulty in the current and getting out of it, and was already as relaxed as a cat in her repose.

'Maybe,' I said sheepishly.

Despite this rather humbling experience, I decided to leave the others to their rest and dry off by going for a walk alone in the forest near our picnic site. Parrots squabbled in overhead branches, their green feathers a perfect match for the leaves, while green and orange rufous-tailed jacamars sallied forth from low perches to nab damselflies. An agouti, the smaller and daintier cousin of the capybara, picked its way delicately through some undergrowth nearby. Life was everywhere, but there was no sign of jaguars. Still, I felt relaxed in the forest in a way most people describe being while lying on a beach, and only reluctantly made my way back to the group, figuring we would push back into the current soon.

We had a lazy, wonderful afternoon puttering on the river, and as dusk set in we came to a place where Marcello said we might see jaguars. Once again, no matter how I resisted it anticipation took hold of me, my relaxed mood dispatched as swiftly as the sun had been.

We beached the boat on a muddy bank with tangled, looping vegetation, the gaps between branches just wide enough to squeeze through. Still barefoot, Marcello led us quietly along the bank, then held up his hand for us to stop. My pulse ratcheted up at the sight before us, and I held my breath.

In the mud in front of us were the clear paw prints of a big cat, and a smoother patch of ground where the cat must have lain down. The edges of the prints were sharp and no insect tracks crossed them, which in this place teeming with life was a sure sign the marks were fresh. A jaguar had been here only moments before. I breathed out, puffing my cheeks, not wanting to get too excited.

'Look there!' Marcello pointed urgently ahead of the tracks we were looking at, and my pulse shot up again. But it was only more tracks—this time, as well as the tracks of an adult there were two smaller sets as well. 'She's got babies!' Marcello whispered to us.

I was initially excited, but then my heart sank. It gets dark suddenly in the tropics, as if a switch has been flicked, and following a jaguar in their prime hunting hours would be beyond dangerous. Add in the mother's natural protectiveness of her cubs, and as foolhardy as I have been in pursuit of animals in the past, even I would have vetoed the idea of trying to approach them on foot. Marcello clearly agreed, and with hand gestures indicated that we should back away until we reached the boat.

'We cannot follow her,' he said. 'Those tracks were so tiny! If we go too close to her babies, she will kill us.'

'Is there a way around?' I asked, desperate hope in my voice.

Marcello pondered, then slowly shook his head. 'Not here, not now. We can try further along in the car later tonight. Maybe they will come out.'

That night we bundled into Marcello's four-wheel drive, and with flashlights pointing from each window and a spotlight mounted at the front, drove along the roads in the area. Capybaras glared at us, moving off the road at the last possible moment, a crab-eating fox trotted gaily along beside us before scurrying into brush, and a raccoon with some small prey in its mouth crossed our beams, but sadly no jaguar emerged.

Even after returning to the campsite I was wired with suspense, and barely slept, excited and frustrated at having been so close to seeing a jaguar only to miss out.

The next day the Minke and I had to move on. We did so with a refreshed outlook on what it means to be lucky, after hearing Marcello's story. It was impossible to be disappointed by our time with him, and I remained optimistic that a jaguar waited for me somewhere down the dirt tracks of South America.

Things I Learnt After the Quake

Together, Parque Machia, Patagonia and the Pantanal had chewed through almost six months of my time in South America. I returned to visit Marguerite and Harris in Santiago, this time with the Minke in tow. As is so often the case when I'm travelling I was broke, and waiting for a royalty payment that was due, so we spent more than a week in Santiago. While we thought we were coming to Santiago for a respite from adventure, fate had other ideas in mind.

Lisa was also happy to have a brief break from life on the road, and we arrived in Santiago grateful for a safe place, a warm and homely base from which we planned to explore the tadpole tail of South America before moving back up into the bulge of Bolivia and Brazil. As previously, I did not expect much from nature in this orderly city. In fact, Chile was so civilised, so well organised, that I'd felt a tinge of selfish disappointment when we decided to return there. The whole reason I had come to South America was to be challenged, to escape the tame, but Santiago felt like Sydney with a Spanish accent. I had no idea it was the place where I would feel nature's force at its greatest, nor a place that would compel me to change my opinions of humanity.

Staying at the Gomezes' also gave Lisa and me some time in a more private setting to explore our new relationship—still in its early, awkward stages. I'd realised the inadvertent danger of sharing a bathroom. I am thrilled that humans have overcome natural selection enough that a woman can find me attractive despite my myriad flaws, and wanted to maintain that honeymoon period for as long as possible.

So it was with some force that I prevented her from brushing her teeth soon after I had left the bathroom one evening. 'Why can't I go in?' she asked. I had no reasonable answer so I said, 'It's haunted.'

'What?'

Realising I'd backed myself into a corner I admitted, 'Okay, not haunted, but it does smell like something died in there.'

'You're a fool,' she replied, pushing past me, and I had an inkling it wouldn't be the last time she said that.

One day during our stay, the Minke and I went to a local bar to watch her beloved Welsh rugby team play France. Wales lost. During the game the Minke revealed a side of her personality I had thus far not witnessed; while never demure, as she watched she became incensed, screaming at the screen, shaking her fist and generally scaring into cautious silence a small cluster of French fans seated nearby.

'Holy crap. My girlfriend is a guy,' I thought but didn't dare say. To reinforce my suspicion, when the game was over she drowned her sorrows with copious volumes of liquor, an amount that even my steel-plated liver couldn't keep pace with, so I didn't try.

•

At 3.34 the next morning I woke, feeling disoriented and confused by a noise I'd never heard before and a world out of control. I grabbed the Minke and insisted she get out of bed.

'I've been through worse,' she insisted—a blatant lie—and rolled over, the mattress bouncing as she did so, not because of her movement but because the whole house was bucking like a bull with an unwanted rider on its back. Time spent in Japan and San Francisco meant that I was familiar with earth tremors, but this was unlike anything I'd experienced before. The windowpanes pulsed violently against their frames, and I could hear waves, a bizarre noise this far from the coast. Later I realised it was the swimming pool, which in daylight revealed itself to be half-full due to the force that had thrown its contents onto the surrounding lawn.

With Lisa reluctantly upright, we staggered towards the bathroom doorframe. A wall came out of nowhere and bounced us to the side, then the opposite wall jabbed us back again. Nothing is as perturbing as being beaten up by a house, but we only had a few paces to go.

'Now you *want* me to go to the bathroom!' the Minke grumbled.

When we reached the doorway I bullied the still-complaining Minke against the frame, and stood panting from the effort and adrenalin. We were on the second floor of the house, and I could see no way of us surviving if the house collapsed, which began to seem increasingly inevitable as the quake continued.

Later I would learn that the quake had lasted just over forty seconds, but at the time it felt like an aeon. I believed that standing in the doorway was our safest option, and slyly figured that any falling objects would land on the Minke before me anyway. (However, after the quake I heard of some controversial research that indicates standing in a doorway or getting under a table may not be the best strategy, as rescuers often find survivors in a 'triangle of life' when they have fallen *beside* a bed or table and a collapsed ceiling hit the

bed first; even if the bed breaks, the person beside it is safe as it tends
to angle over them.)

'I'm going out to check on the others,' I said once the shaking
had subsided.

Lisa, who was either still drunk or suicidally forlorn over her
rugby team's loss, said, 'I'm going back to bed.' And she did, maintaining a far straighter line to it than before.

I heard voices in the hallway and found the entire family Gomez—
Harris, Marguerite and their two daughters—gathered in various
states of pyjamery outside the cluster of bedrooms that made up the
house's upper floor.

'Why is the house driving?' the five-year-old asked, a beautiful
description of the grinding pulses we had just felt. Marguerite had
tears in her eyes and was still shaking visibly. Harris asked after Lisa,
and I explained she was back in bed.

'She's tough,' said Harris, eyebrows raised in admiration.

'Drunk actually, but how are all of you?' I replied.

Once we'd ascertained that everyone was fine, Harris and I went
off to check if there was any damage to the house. The electricity was
out, and when we turned to look out the window the view stunned
us both. The house was built on the side of a dormant volcano, and
overlooked a valley that stretched into central Santiago. Usually the
city winked and sparkled at night; now there was nothing but the
occasional red flare of an emergency light. There was nothing to tell us
whether a city of seven million people still stood. In the gloom around
us all that was clear was that a neighbour's house remained upright,
but it was impossible to know what had happened beyond that.

Sirens started, one by one, and far below us some headlights
wended their way in a serpentine fashion that made me think they

must be avoiding rubble. Later I learnt that many of the lights I saw were people hastily making their way home to loved ones—it was a Friday night after all, and Latinos start partying late and finish even later.

'What do you think is going on out there?' Harris asked.

'No idea,' I said, wishing there was more light but suspecting from the sheer force of the shake that we would be without electricity for some time. The quake was the most powerful sensation I had ever experienced, and while the shaking continued I had felt more impotent than ever before. But it occurred to me now that I should go out and see if there was a way I could be of help to anyone. There would be death out there, I knew, but how much? The quake that had rocked Haiti around a month earlier had claimed over one hundred thousand lives. Images from that disaster also made me worry about looters. The Gomezes' house is beautiful, and perhaps only the well-built homes of the wealthy would now remain standing. While I wouldn't begrudge anyone searching for food or shelter I knew that a disaster could bring out the very worst in human nature. As Harris and I trudged back to the second floor I privately decided that the top of the stairs would be our best line of defence should anyone break in.

There wasn't much I could do until sunrise, but I lay awake for several hours after I went back to bed. Just before dawn, there was a sound like an angry ocean, and a second later the house began to shake again. Once again, the windows flexed far more than I thought glass could, and the bed bounced as if a giant was jumping on it (though the Minke was asleep).

'I felt that one,' she said, waking as I got up.

'Hard not to,' I replied, finally agreeing with Harris that Lisa was tough, as she was clearly more stoic than I and determined to sleep through this event. I kissed her cheek and again went out into the hall and joined the family.

'Not as big as the first,' said Harris.

'Nope. Don't think so,' I agreed.

'How many more will there be?' Marguerite asked.

Again, I had no idea. I knew that earthquakes were caused by tectonic plates pushing against each other until the build-up forced one to slip over, under, or alongside the other, and that Santiago sat right on the junction between two such plates. In 1960 it had experienced the most powerful earthquake since records began, at 9.5 on the Richter scale, so devastating that most of the city had had to be rebuilt. What I learnt after our earthquake was that Chile had subsequently instituted one of the world's strictest building codes, and actually adhered to it. But looking over the darkened valley it was impossible to know how successful they had been. Only dawn would tell.

Tremors came through the last dark hours, and through the morning, triggering howls from every neighbourhood dog except the Gomezes' loafing cocker spaniel, who for no reason apart from probable stupidity just ignored the entire affair.

With light came the discovery that the only apparent damage to the house was a gas bottle that had torn loose from some flimsy mounts and would be easily fixed. A walk through the neighbourhood showed our reprieve was no one-off miracle; apart from broken glass and zigzagging cracks in roads there was no significant damage. Only later would we find out that some of the few buildings that had survived the 1960 quake had been damaged or destroyed fifty years later, unable to take a second blow.

Within six hours of the initial quake the electricity was back on. The internet took only twelve hours to be reconnected. The local supermarket stayed shut for a day as the staff put everything that had fallen off the shelves back on (I imagined them watching forlornly each time aftershocks toppled everything off again), and the ATMs all ran out of money as people made panic withdrawals. Nevertheless, by Monday it was all systems go—stores open, banks operating, food available. I had faced greater inconveniences in Africa without any natural disasters involved.

The media was painting a different picture, however. While what we could see from our windows seemed secure enough, it was hard to get reliable information about other places the quake might have hit. We gathered around the television as soon as the power was back on and were surprised to learn that Santiago was in flames, the city destroyed; as bad as that sounded, Concepción to the south was even worse, reporters claimed.

'They're pretty much saying we're dead,' I said. 'I feel fine though.'

It was the worst sort of sensationalist reporting. Concepción, it was true, was far worse hit than the capital, but Santiago got a black eye, and was never knocked down. Oft-repeated footage showed the army beating a looter, but close observation showed he was stealing a television, and a woman behind him taking bread from a supermarket was given free passage. Within days I began to see a national spirit that I had never encountered anywhere else before. Chileans rallied to help their fellow countrymen, in ways small and large. Cars were painted with the slogan '*Fuerza*, Chile!' (Strength, Chile!), and teens—who I usually (and cynically) believe are only good for pimple-milking for oil—volunteered inside supermarkets, asking customers if they would buy items such as milk formula or tinned food that could be donated outside for distribution to people in need. Normally if there is any animal that I would claim to dislike it is my own species, but in Santiago after the quake I found myself with a permanent lump in my throat at the solidarity being shown.

•

Two weeks later Lisa's parents, at her urging, came to visit. We all felt the best way we could help was to put money into the economy and let others know that Chile was dealing with the problem better than an outsider might imagine. We drove the Minke's parents along the Pan-American Highway, Chile's major artery, and saw sights that staggered her father, an engineer, who was able to fully appreciate how well roads and buildings had withstood the violence, and how quickly infrastructure was being tended to.

'I don't believe it,' Papa Minke said one day as we drove along. 'I've never seen that in the UK!'

I scanned around for things I imagined would be unfamiliar to UKsians, such as a shower or winning sports team, but saw none.

'There were four guys standing in a hole back there, and instead of just one guy working and three "supervising", all four had shovels and were hard at it!' he explained.

In the wrecked town of Linares we witnessed the greatest destruction wrought by the earthquake. Adobe houses had tumbled to the ground, and the church's steeple was far from plumb. Incredibly no deaths had been reported in Linares itself, but the greater Maule region it is a part of had experienced the highest toll from the quake. Despite this there was no wailing, just hard work going on. There was nowhere to stay in Linares, so we bought some supplies there and drove on until we reached Chillán. It took some searching, but we found a small hostel that was open, where the apologetic owner explained that the water service was unreliable, but offered us a discounted rate for the rooms.

We refused the discount, stayed the night, then pushed on the next morning, passing huge groups of volunteers who were busy building shelters or distributing food. This worst of disasters had brought out the best in people, and I felt a little guilty that on the night of the quake I had been so concerned about looters.

During our two-week-long tour of Chile details began to emerge of just how powerful the quake had been. At the epicentre it had registered as 8.8 on the Richter scale, with a reading of 8 in Santiago. Its effects had been felt as far away as New Orleans. The city of Concepción had moved a staggering three metres from where it used to be, Santiago twenty-seven centimetres. Even Buenos Aires, on the other side of the Andes, had shifted four centimetres. South America's tail had wagged, making maps of the world subtly wrong. The quake had been so violent that the Earth had shifted slightly on its axis, shortening the length of the day by a fraction of a second.

The only way I could conceptualise this was to think of a picnic blanket laid out with food, glasses and drinks, then wondering if I could drag it twenty-seven centimetres without anything falling over. Imagining it that way made me realise how incredible it was that anything had stayed standing, and how lucky we had been.

The Family Minke and I carried on with our travels into regions that geography had spared from any damage. We attracted many stares along the way; at first I attributed this to us being the first tourists people had seen in weeks, before realising that as a group we probably looked like a lesson in genetics. Papa Minke is a slim but commanding six foot three, Mama Minke comes in at a statuesque five-eleven, and the Minke herself fits evenly between at six-one. My five feet nine presumably made me look like their pet koala.

It was my second time to some of the regions we visited, but this time around I was able to look at them with fresh eyes. Whereas when I first arrived in Chile I was disappointed by its civilisation and order, now I realised how selfish my earlier disappointment had been. I would never wish poor living standards on anyone, but I had been a little disappointed in how developed Chile was. Bolivia had felt more like the South America I expected—ramshackle, fetid and berserk—while Chile felt more like an outpost of Europe. I could not begrudge Chileans their advancement, and seeing the way they had dealt with the savage blow of the earthquake I now admired and respected the people of this country enormously.

But the most important lesson for me had come on the very morning of the quake, as we sat eating breakfast, bread toasted over a gas grill while we waited for the electricity to come back on. Without Chile's economic development things would have been so different. I had the Minke with me, and my feelings for her grew stronger every day. But I also had Harris and Marguerite and their brood, as close to family as we could be without sharing DNA, and seeing them safe and unharmed made me very, very glad.

Fuerza, Chile.

Getting High in Bolivia

Sometimes travel can be testing but the tests bring great rewards. At other times, though, travel is like testing your breath by getting someone to kick you in the nose. That was how I felt after getting off a flight from London that had come to Santiago via Dallas, with little time to do anything other than wash off the travel sauce and brush my teeth before getting onto a bus scheduled for a twenty-three-hour trip to San Pedro de Atacama, a small town close to the Chile–Bolivia border in the world's driest desert.

I'd been in London to promote my last book; after a fortnight of wearing ironed clothes and shoes that shone, I immediately felt more at ease in rumpled T-shirts and battered sneakers. Despite how remarkably comfortable and clean Chilean buses are, I rarely sleep on them, but as this one lurched away from the terminal my eyes began an inexorable droop, and soon I was drooling onto the headrest of the unfortunate passenger beside me.

A few times that night I woke, slurped, apologised, then fell asleep once more, but on the whole I had a not unpleasant trip, waking properly as sunbeams pierced chinks in the drawn curtains, and passengers got up and queued for the loo at the back. I went to stand, but found that I no longer had any joints in my legs. After more than forty-eight hours sitting down on buses and planes, my knees had apparently left me for a younger man, and only unlocked with a noise like a giant crushing rocks. Outside, the view had changed from Santiago's sculpted lawns and office blocks to true desert, a place where rain was so rare that a few drops could wash away roads that weren't built to deal with moisture and would have been deadly—if anyone actually lived here.

Anyone, that is, apart from miners. The road swept past occasional mining operations, the tailings piled in pyramids that evoked the men's Inca ancestors, strange mineral colours swirling through the rock like ice-cream toppings.

Finally reaching San Pedro, I acknowledged the tightening of a headache, that had built as the bus climbed through the desert to this mountain town. Headaches rarely afflict me except on mornings after red wine. This was no hangover though, and it was paired with a shortness of breath. San Pedro sits at just under two and a half thousand metres, so the oxygen content is significantly lower than Santiago at a mere four hundred and fifty metres, or London, which cruises along at sea level. With protesting lungs I trawled the town for the hostel I was booked into, scanning local maps seemingly designed to baffle visitors and lead them past every possible place but the one they were looking for.

When I finally found the hostel I was surprised that the Minke wasn't there waiting for me. She'd been booked on a bus from Argentina, where she'd spent the last two weeks viewing its wine regions. Eventually she arrived, accompanied by a local man on a bicycle. 'We met at the bus stop,' Lisa told me, 'and he insisted on helping me find the hostel.' She shot me a remarkably articulate glance that said, 'No, I am not picking up stray human beings; he wouldn't leave me alone.' The man clearly suffered some powerful delusions (perhaps a life with little oxygen had taken its toll), and

while twitching, insisted that the town was not safe, and that it was
a combination of New York and Miami. ('Have you been to either?'
I asked. 'No,' he replied, confirming what I'd suspected.) He seemed
to want to offer his services as a guide, or bodyguard; while one of
his eyes rolled in random directions I politely refused his offer, and
thanked him for helping the Minke. Once he'd wobbled off on his
bike I was aghast when Lisa said she wanted to press on the next
day into Bolivia. She had had a hellacious journey that had included
a three-hour wait at the Argentinian border, but was eager to keep
moving. Meanwhile I was all for some R&R.

'You can rest when you're dead,' she pointed out, and even though
it felt like that state might come about sooner rather than later I
agreed to the plan.

So the next day, still tasting airline food between my teeth,
I trudged with Lisa to a tourist office and booked a three-day trip
into Bolivia. We'd been warned that many of the operators who
offered this trip were shonky, but a friend had recommended one
company and it was with some relief that I saw there was a little tread
on the tyres of the four-wheel-drive Toyota LandCruiser we boarded
later that morning.

There were six of us plus a driver in the LandCruiser, which
had incongruous T-Rex decals on the windscreen. In this chariot
we would wend our way over the Andes into Bolivia, then across
the world's largest salt flats to a town called Uyuni.

We had a near-disastrous start. On the outskirts of San Pedro we
cleared immigration procedure to exit Chile, then headed into
no-man's land where we climbed, climbed and climbed some more,
the dry landscape punctuated by occasional bursts of mineral colour
and the even more unlikely sight of high-altitude springs with lurid

green and red algae, speckled with the pink of feeding flamingos. Then, just as incompatible with the surrounds, we sighted a solitary shack, and beside it a flagpole from which the brightly coloured Bolivian flag snapped in the strong wind. All we had to do here was get our passports stamped and carry on, a simple procedure in most places. There was just one problem. The Minke.

'What is this country?' the border guard asked in Spanish, looking at the Minke's passport. Lisa had written '*Gales*' on her form, the Spanish word for Wales. She explained that it was near England, and was part of the United Kingdom, like Scotland.

'It is not a real country,' the guard said, crossing out '*Gales*' and writing '*Inglatera*' beside it.

Of course, the Welsh and English, despite being neighbours and ruled by the same parliament, have a contentious history that includes acts of colonial bastardry by the English that have not been forgotten by the Welsh. Calling a Welshman English is not the greatest insult imaginable, but may cost you some teeth if the Welsh person in question feels sufficiently aggrieved by it. As the Minke straightened to her full and imposing height, I started to fear we might just see the inside of a Bolivian jail before the day was out, so I grabbed her and said, 'Choose your battles.'

She glared at me.

'Of course Wales is a real country, he just can't be expected to know that, what with Bolivia not playing rugby,' I said.

She didn't look convinced.

'They don't have schools here either,' I added facetiously.

She laughed then and we were stamped in, and in no time we were back in the vehicle, shivering from our brief exposure to the bitter mountain air.

The temperature had gone from pleasant and sun-soaked in San Pedro to a harsh, windswept chill now that we had hit three and a half thousand metres. As the vehicle climbed further we passed larger lakes with the occasional pause for photos. Small herds of vicuñas scattered at our approach, their daintiness in stark contrast to their more famous relative, the camel. The lakes themselves were so saturated with naturally occurring minerals that the water ranged from red to green, with shades of blue and orange in between.

Despite their toxic appearance, each lake had a population of flamingos working the water, avocets too, and many smaller birds that took off before I could get close enough to identify them, probably alerted by my harsh panting. Every step up there felt like a marathon, and just climbing a rocky outcrop for a better view left me wrecked, condor bait—if there had been any condors around. This was without a doubt the most inhospitable place I had ever been to. Parts of this mountain range had never recorded rain, and temperatures ranged from scorching in the lowlands to the breath-fogging cold of the spring-fed lakes.

Our group was all European, apart from myself and Eduoardo, our driver, who was Bolivian. The Minke was, as noted, proudly Welsh, there was a French girl, a softly spoken young German man with spiky dyed-red hair, and a Polish couple. The Polish couple spoke no Spanish, but the woman had some understanding of English, so that—conveniently for me—became the common language.

'Can you breathe?' I asked the Polish woman as she stumbled up onto the rock beside me. All she did was pant in reply, waving at her mouth to indicate she couldn't speak. So I guessed not. Not only had I not been at altitude for some time, I had never before been quite so high. Australia and Botswana, the countries where I have spent most time, are both markedly flat, their highest peaks mere pimples on the landscape compared to the Andes. I was struggling.

There's a certain sheer bloody-mindedness that comes with being a bird watcher, that seemingly most passive of activities, and so when we reached our final destination for the day, the azure Lago Colorado, I was determined to get out there and see what new species I could spot from its shores. Lago Colorado is one of the only places on the globe where three species of flamingo can be seen, as well as many specialist high-altitude species with eponymous names like Andean goose, Andean avocet, and gasping foolfinch. (One of those names might have been made up while addled by lack of oxygen.)

There was nowhere near enough water in the vehicle for the group, and the dehydrating caffeinated drink the driver constantly sipped on would do me no favours, so I took what water could be spared and set off on what I thought would be a leisurely stroll. The flamingos were easy to find, as were several of the other larger species. It amazed me how diverse the bird life was—we had peaked here at four and a half thousand metres, a punishing altitude for anything with lungs, yet I easily saw twenty species of birds in a few hundred metres. For some reason, though, I was convinced that on the other side of the lake, only a half-kilometre around, would be more species that I had not seen before. There was no logical reason for this, but like many enthusiasts, bird watchers can become irrationally fixated. So I stumbled along, mouth open, ignoring the dizziness I felt and the weakness in my legs. A drab brown bird called a cinclodes lifted off in front of me, so plain that it could only delight the most hardened bird nerd; I was sufficiently inspired at this sight to carry on.

A natural spring fed the lake, and I soon found its outlet, which was bright green with algae. I was thirsty, having finished the bottle of water I'd brought, but feared drinking from even this most pure of natural sources might turn me green, like an anorexic Hulk.

I pushed on, spotting a few more species, my shoes now coated with dust as I could only drag my feet, not lift them. Eventually it dawned on me how stupid I was being—a remarkable moment of clarity considering how foolishly I'd been behaving to that point. I could barely breathe, and a mere stroll had me close to collapse. Now I had to get back.

As I looked over the flamingo-coated lake, our camp, less than a kilometre away, suddenly seemed impossibly far. I groaned, made a shuffling turn, and started retracing the drag marks my feet had left. 'I'm too old for this,' I thought, returning to my new favourite theme. This time though I didn't mean I was too old for adventure, but too old for such stupidity. Getting back seemed improbable; doing it before blinding dark certainly so. The sky was turning the same shade of pink as the flamingos, and there was no source of artificial light between me and the camp. This was no place to spend the night and wait it out—exposure could kill up here, and soon I wouldn't even have the energy to shiver.

I began dragging my feet again, a shambling figure. I'd told Lisa that I was going for a walk, but had neglected to mention exactly where I intended to go. How long would it be before they sent someone to look for me? If they had hardly any water in the car, would they have flashlights? This was not Chile but Bolivia, the country I'd expected to find in South America—undoubtedly charming, but chaotic and ramshackle. I felt such a fool as the light faded, too exhausted now to even lift my binoculars at what might have been a bird but was probably just an hallucination, the product of an oxygen-starved mind.

The lake edge had a gentle curve that I needed to follow back to the camp, with an ill-defined trail following the arc. I decided to cut a corner, but soon realised the folly of that as I sank almost to my ankles in rich, gluggy mud, weighing down my feet further. I was torn between the need to hurry to beat the setting sun and conserving energy by moving at a less lung-busting pace. From the outside I must have looked like an arthritic tortoise, but I felt even more decrepit. Earlier I had found the lack of oxygen and its effects a novelty—not pleasant, but a new experience and therefore worth savouring. Now it scared me. I felt like I was drowning on land.

One step, then another. I paused, leant over and rubbed my thighs. They ached, deep aches as though I'd run a marathon (not that I know from experience what that's like). My mini-break over, I started moving again, making it only a few paces before stopping once more, my breathing now rapid and harsh, like a horny bull elephant that has spotted a breeding herd.

In the distance I saw a light come on, and realised it was from the arrangement of huts that made up our campsite. It was still distant, too distant, and it hit me that I wasn't going to make it. The will that had driven me forward to see some different birds was absent now. And, incredibly, making it through the night was not as powerful a motivator. I sometimes joked that my lack of coordination disproved the theory of evolution, and my lack of will to survive now made it quite clear that this was true.

I pushed on as soon as I felt able to do so, the light now a beacon, drawing me towards it. I stumbled into some more mud, my shoes now leaden lumps. I seriously considered dropping to my hands and knees and crawling. Instead I shook my feet, one after the other; though the energy that took almost winded me, I broke into a stumbling trot, making it at least twelve paces before tripping and falling onto all fours, shuffling a while this way before getting up again and, with some newfound will, taking a few more steps.

After a while the light seemed closer, brighter, and I considered shouting but doubted my voice would be any louder than a strangled fart. I stumbled along, my throat raw from dragging at the thin air. It was a ragged figure that stumbled into the communal room and collapsed onto the bed assigned for me.

'You okay?' the Minke asked me, looking up from her book.

'No,' I said, but before I could elaborate it became apparent from some squeaks and creaks that the Polish couple, not at all mindful of being in a well-lit room with four other people, were engaged in some under-the-blanky hanky-panky. It was hard to believe anyone could have the energy for that under the circumstances; I didn't think I could even muster the strength to laugh at it, but then a choked guffaw emerged that I tried to stifle with my hand. Soon the Minke and I must have looked as if we were engaged in the same activity as we clutched at each other to try to muffle our giggles.

•

Waking the next morning I looked out at the lake and berated myself for being a drama queen. It really wasn't that far to the other side. But after taking my first few steps of the morning my legs went dead and my head pulsed with flares of pain behind each eye.

Mountains are not my thing, I decided: I can't ski (apparently I was born without a pelvis, as my legs drift apart as soon as I set off on skis and simply will not rejoin), I don't like the cold, and while flamingos are all very nice, I prefer the jungle, where being a bird watcher might get me killed by something like a jaguar, but at least that had some dignity to it. We had three more days of travel ahead of us, and then some time scheduled in La Paz, perched at an altitude greater than any other capital city in the world. After that it was all downhill to the jungle, and there'd be no more getting high for me.

Driving Blind with Jesus

There's an old saying in Africa that goes something like this: 'You're a bloody idiot, Peter Allison.' Like many old sayings there is much truth to it, which may explain why I became so excited at the idea of spending five days floating down a tributary of the Amazon on tyre tubes. Lisa and I were in the office of a small tour company, and I hopped from foot to foot like a child with a full bladder, while the Minke, sensible and therefore unsure as to whether the trip was a good idea, prevaricated. Another option was to take a motorised canoe, in which case the same journey could be done in three days. However, that seemed incurably dull to me, and when I added wheedling and puppy eyes to my full-bladder dance, the Minke agreed to go the tyre-tube route. Before she could change her mind, we booked in.

We were in La Paz, the world's highest capital city, but since my evening of birdwatching at Lago Colorado, I'd become somewhat more acclimatised and the hilly streets only punished me mildly for daring to walk them.

We decided to fill in the few days until the trip began by heading to the small town of Coroico, a few hours downhill from La Paz. The Minke decided to make her way there on a mountain bike, riding along the infamous Death Road, a path with sheer drops that has claimed many lives. My fear of heights precluded me from enjoying such an activity, so instead I took a minivan along a newer, only moderately more sane piece of engineering that was deadly looking for a mere fifty per cent of the time.

After arriving in Coroico via our different routes and modes of transport, the Minke and I relaxed for a few days. Then the power went out, resulting in the whole town's electricity being switched off. This was clearly such a common occurrence that everyone continued with business as usual, all with a stock of candles at hand. Unfortunately, we were waiting to hear from the tyre-tube people via email about a blockade that might make our departure impossible. Truck drivers, unhappy with some government figure, had blocked several routes out of La Paz, and were beating up any drivers who tried to get through. They were apparently tolerant of foreigners and might let them pass, but the situation could flare up at any moment.

For hours we waited; finally, as the sun dipped beneath the omnipresent Andes and plunged us into gloom, the sound of refrigerators kicking into gear and lights dimly glowing told us that the town's power was back on. Scurrying back to the internet café we logged on to find a message saying that yes, we were going ahead with the trip, and that the company had a blockade-busting plan in place. All we had to do was be back in La Paz the next day for a five am departure, instead of the previously arranged and far more civilised start time of ten.

'Buggershitpisswee,' I said. 'We'd have to leave here at two!' We found a working phone and to our surprise someone was still in the tour office back in La Paz. Whereas in the West many such places might have been inflexible with regard to our predicament, the man on the other end merely said, 'Ah, no problem, we will leave later, how about eight?'

So it was that at four the next morning, we waited bleary-eyed for a taxi we'd arranged the day before to take us back to La Paz. Shortly after we were climbing the switchback road, leaving the pleasant vegetation of Coroico behind for the stripped-bare mountainsides surrounding the ramshackle capital.

•

When Lisa and I booked the tyre-tube trip we'd been the only people interested, but we arrived back in La Paz to find the tour had filled up with six more people who would be joining us. They slowly assembled: a young English guy named Nick, an Israeli ('Call me David,' he said. 'Not Ishmael?' I asked facetiously, paraphrasing *Moby-Dick*. 'No,' he replied. 'My name is Adair. But call me David'), an Italian woman named Gabriela, a Dutch couple, and a Spanish man named Thema with a bald and mottled scalp, who was the only person visibly older than me.

'Okay, folks, here is the deal,' said the man from the office, who spoke remarkably good English. 'We cannot get through the blockade.'

My heart sank. Had we left Coroico at the crack of dawn for nothing?

'But we can go around it,' he continued. 'It will add a day to the trip, which we won't charge you for, okay?'

We all agreed, happy that our adventure hadn't been cancelled.

'Instead of taking just a few hours to get to the river, it will be a seven-hour drive, and I'll admit that the vehicle is not the most comfortable, but it is the best we can do. Is everyone happy with that?'

'Seven hours, not a problem,' I thought. 'Sure,' I said.

Sure, the others all agreed.

The vehicle, another four-wheel drive, was built to take only seven passengers, but there were eight of us, plus the guide we met at the office just prior to departure. His name was Cesar, pronounced 'Chazar', and he was a deep-voiced man with the weathered features of someone who'd lived most of his life outdoors.

'And this,' Cesar intoned in his bass rumble, 'is our driver, Jesus.'

'Holy Roman Empire,' I thought.

Jesus (pronounced 'Heyzuz') turned out to be a taciturn man who kept a bag of coca leaves stashed beside him. Coca (the raw material from which cocaine is manufactured) is perfectly legal in Bolivia, and at any given time more people than not seem to have wads of it in their cheeks, chewing it for the mild buzz it provides, and for its supposed benefits of increased concentration and alertness. Personally, I found it made my mouth taste of leaves and did little else except make my gums a little numb, which meant I spilled even more than usual of whatever I was drinking.

We piled in, and everyone agreed that the Minke should get the front seat with its greater leg room, as she was clearly the tallest of our group. I was scrunched in the narrowest seat at the back with the Dutch couple, a friendly pair who had the blemish-free skin of people who lived healthily and rarely saw the sun. In front of me in a tight knot sat the four singletons, and we all chatted merrily as Jesus set off through the choked roads of La Paz. A wheel well that pressed into my buttock rendered my right leg numb almost immediately, but seven hours would be fine, I was sure. To ensure blood reached my foot I would just need to occasionally shift around as if breaking wind.

We soon left the winding mountain roads and hit the broad, open altiplano. These high-altitude plains have been agricultural lands since the Incas, and are still tended by poncho-wearing Quichua people, accompanied by bored-looking llamas.

As soon as we hit the flat plains Jesus put his foot down, continuing to chew monotonously on his coca. While we were travelling on one of these long stretches there was a sudden bang and our momentum abruptly decreased before the vehicle started to lurch about. I felt a clawed hand clutch my thigh and thought it belonged to one of the Dutch, then realised it was my own. We veered off the road, coming to a skidding halt some metres from the tarmac, where we all got out of the vehicle.

As a guide I'd changed countless tyres so I offered to help, just to give my still-shaking hands something to do. My offer was rejected and instead I threw one arm around Lisa, who I feared might already be regretting coming on this trip with me. Jesus and Cesar got to work changing the tyre, and recommended we walk to the town a kilometre down the road, where they would join us for lunch.

The air was chilly, but we were all keen for a walk to stretch our legs, and the views were so spectacular nobody much noticed the cold. We were in an elevated valley, and from the dead-flat altiplano the Andes loomed on each side of us, rising to impossibly high snow-capped peaks.

Only a few minutes down the road we were sprayed with dust as Jesus skidded to a stop in front of our strolling group, and urged us back into the vehicle. After a bland café lunch of maize soup and a meat probably best left unidentified, we were on the road again.

By now we'd been driving for about three hours, and my back was already jarred from the uneven road and my right leg was so numb it felt detachable, so I was comforted by the thought that we must be close to halfway through the journey. So when Cesar said, without explanation, that the journey might take ten hours, we were all moved to a frozen silence, broken only when, for no discernible reason, Thema started singing a few lines of a Spanish song in a deep off-key voice, before muttering something unintelligible.

We had ended up leaving La Paz at ten in the morning, so the original estimate of seven hours would have had us at our tyre-tube launching point at around five in the evening, maybe as late as seven allowing for the usual elasticity in Bolivian estimates of time. But Cesar bumping up the total trip time by another three hours made me wonder if we'd be on the road far longer again. Periodically I postured up, had a shake-shake of what my mama gave me, and settled back down, bloodflow assured for the next little while. To pass the time I started a sweepstake: the estimates of our arrival time ranged from the Dutch couple's optimistic seven pm, through to my cynical one am.

As it turned out we were all optimists, and getting through the night would be one of the most frightening experiences I've ever had.

•

We left the altiplano in the mid-afternoon and were soon on pure mountain roads again, a mix of dry dirt and gravel that pinged against the bottom of the vehicle, the dust kicked up by the tyres permeating the leaky seals and forming a paste in our mouths. There were few other cars to be seen, but plenty of trucks, which flew past us on the narrow roads at suicidal speeds, rocking our four-wheel drive on its springs with a blast of wind and a toot of the horn, then enveloping us in blinding dust. Although unable to see through the dust, Jesus wouldn't even slow down; he just drove on at the same pace until we emerged at the other side, miraculously still on the road and not flying off one of the sheer cliffs above which the road wound.

'*Murciélago* . . . what is *murciélago* in English?' Cesar muttered from the front at one point, his voice so deep it carried all the way to the back. While my Spanish was still far from expert, one of the first things I learn in any language are animal names, so I was able to reply, 'Bat.'

'Yes! Bat! Who wants to see a bat?' Cesar rumbled pleasantly.

The other passengers and I all looked at each other blankly. Though the idea of a break from the cramped interior was appealing, I was also keen to reach our destination within a reasonable time. When I said this everyone murmured their assent, which left us nowhere. We needed a leader.

'I need to stretch my legs,' the Minke said, and so it was decided.

We turned off the road we were on, the only pass through this section of the mountain yet so narrow it was impossible to believe it was a 'main' road. After travelling down what felt like a goat track, Jesus stopped the vehicle near the entrance to a cave, where for a paltry entry fee we were shown some stalagmites, stalactites, and bats that looked down at us with an indifference that possibly mirrored our own.

'Nobody knows where this water goes,' Cesar intoned, gesturing towards a decent-sized body of water covering much of the base of the cave. 'According to legend, the Incas used to throw golden idols in here, along with human sacrifices, to please the gods. Lots of people have looked for the gold, and some have tried to explore further to find out where the water goes. The last group to do so were Japanese. None of them came back.'

I felt the creepy tingle a good story can produce and was also glad to be out of the cramped vehicle, but that was all Cesar had for us and in a short time we were herded back to where Jesus was waiting, and squeezed back into his chariot. After heading back up the goat track we rejoined the main road, but the two roads met at an angle that meant we were facing the wrong way. Any sensible driver would have continued along a little distance until they found a section wide enough to do a three-point turn.

Jesus didn't.

With no discernible change in the rate of his cud chewing, he yanked strongly on the wheel and we slewed sideways, just as we had when the tyre had blown, and nudged into the gently sloping bank that defined one side of the road. The other side was more abrupt, dropping several hundred screaming metres to life-eating rocks below.

Jesus backed up towards the edge of the cliff.

I have two default behaviours when scared, each aimed at distracting myself from whatever it is that frightens me. One is to make the crazed grunting of an aroused baboon and the other is to be sarcastic. This time I found myself reverting to sarcasm. 'Oh goody, Jesus thinks he can drive on air,' I said.

The Dutch girl looked at me through eyes glazed with terror, clearly wondering how I could be flippant at a time like this.

We stopped suddenly, lurched forward again towards the bank, then shot back once more. This would be no three-point turn. Oh no, this was going to take several bites to get through, and each one was making my internal organs squirm. Finally we got to a point where we were exactly ninety degrees to the road. Heart thudding, I prayed a truck wouldn't come barrelling along and, unable to stop in time, smash us straight off the ledge; on the other hand, Jesus's driving might get us there first.

He reversed again, aiming for maximum turning room, taking the rear wheels right to the lip of the ledge. Everyone remained silent, except the Dutch guy, who gave a strangled groan. I didn't want to look out the window, but my neck swivelled of its own accord. Through the narrow aperture that was the rearmost window I could see down. Straight down, to the base of the cliff which was strewn with mangled cars, trucks and buses. For a brief moment I wished I was blind. We were over nothing but air, and I damn near pooped.

'You okay back there?' the Minke asked, not turning around to do so.

'No,' I squeaked.

Gravel crunched and I was sure the lip we were on was about to give way, and that we would tumble and freefall to an excruciating death. This road made the Death Road seem wimpy.

But Jesus revved the engine, and after several more scrotum-withering turns we were facing in the desired direction and we zoomed off, the sound of the engine almost drowned by a collective exhalation.

Our relief was short-lived and a general grumpiness set in as the road rocked and rattled us, those trying to snooze cracking their skulls against windows or the heads of others as the vehicle bumped and thumped along the corrugated track. We were still in the high Andes, and every time I took heart from a descent any hope was soon dispelled by a steep climb.

The seven-hour mark we had been promised passed, then the revised ten hours. My right leg no longer felt like it had ever belonged to me. The Dutch couple and I played a game of musical chairs in the cramped back seat. It might possibly have been erotic under other circumstances, but we did it purely to stop gangrene setting in from lack of bloodflow.

'How much longer now?' English Nick asked about eleven hours into our journey.

'Another two, maybe three hours,' Cesar rumbled, not even attempting to soften the blow.

'Jesus,' somebody muttered, but the driver didn't respond.

'La, lahlahlah!' Thema sang, which was odd but not particularly disturbing as by this time I thought I might be going mad too. One of my knees had been wedged into a nostril (not my own) for some time and a seatbelt socket that had been broken off dug into the small of my back, gouging into it with every jolt.

Finally we were granted another break, not due to the kindness of Cesar or Jesus but because the car was overheating, understandable in the circumstances. We stopped in a village, where we ate at a small restaurant, grumbling to one another through the meal, feeling we had been lied to.

'My legs are so sore,' the Minke said, rubbing at her lengthy limbs. 'But I can't uncurl them or I'll end up in Cesar's lap.'

'Yeah, I'd prefer you didn't do that,' I said, not out of any real jealousy, but because Cesar on occasion fed coca directly to Jesus so he didn't have to take his hands off the wheel. I had a theory that the coca might be all that was keeping him awake and the four-wheel drive on the road.

Back in the vehicle, Cesar turned to us. 'Only four hours to go now,' he said.

'What?!' exclaimed the Minke in dismay.

'Yes, we are close now!' Cesar replied, clearly delighted.

Meanwhile, Jesus just kept on chewing and steering and pushing the throttle, driving us into darkness barely pierced by his headlights, until a truck came by, sheeting us in dust which didn't seem to lift no matter how much further on we drove. After a while I realised it wasn't dust hanging infinitely in the air but a fog that had descended, dense and cooling. This was good for the engine, but I rescinded my earlier wish for blindness and hoped that Jesus had been endowed with X-ray vision. As it was we were driving blind without a guide dog, and it was madness.

The fear that overcame us all during Jesus's earlier lunatic turnaround came back, and silence again dominated the vehicle. Even Thema stopped treating us to fragments of songs none of us knew.

From the back seat I could see only a portion of the windscreen, blocked as it was by the row in front of me, and Jesus, Cesar and the Minke (whose head was oddly angled to avoid hitting the roof), but what I could see was the most frightening vista of opacity, just a blank nothing, as if the world had ended.

'Keep feeding that man coca!' I shouted, breaking the silence, hoping that the leaves would somehow impart laser-like vision to Jesus. 'He must know this road really well,' I tried to tell myself. 'So well that he doesn't even need to see it!'

Soon after this wishful thinking of mine we lurched to a halt once more, ten heads rocking forward then snapping back with the sudden deceleration. Jesus reversed a little, then made a sharp left turn. It took a moment to register what had happened, before it dawned on me that we'd almost driven straight off a cliff. Jesus wasn't driving by memory, radar or supernatural powers, he was just peering into the gloom and had only seen the turn a split second before it was too late.

Less than an hour later lights appeared ahead of us, not moving; as we drew closer I saw it was a small *pueblo* (a vague term meaning more than one hut, but smaller than a town) with electricity from a generator. Several buses were parked in the *pueblo*'s small scrubby parking lot, their passengers sleeping through the break. But we powered on by, making me more and more terrified. Bolivian buses are famously dangerous, with a safety record comparable to asbestos mining, so if other bus drivers had pulled over because of the poor visibility then continuing on was surely as safe as juggling chainsaws while blow-drying your hair in a shark tank.

●

It was nearly two am and we'd been travelling for fourteen hours when we finally started to descend. Down, down, we went, down and down, so that I felt we must've finally punctured the Andes and would start heading into the lowlands, where the jungle and river began.

I was right. Less than an hour later we burst from the fog into fetid and humid air, air that had oxygen in it, and a tang. It smelled of bananas, papaya and other, more exotic fruits, and pricked sweat beads from the skin. The change was no less dramatic than waking up to find you'd turned into a kangaroo. Spontaneous conversation began, jaws unclenched, fists unballed, shoulders relaxed, and Thema sang a snatch of song before breaking into his standard encore of unintelligible muttering.

Three hours later the euphoria of survival had worn off, and it was a grubby, grumbling bunch of travellers who disembarked from Jesus's jalopy in a bland little town somewhere between two places not marked on any maps. The muss-haired woman we'd woken up at the town's hostel was surprisingly chirpy for the hour, and with good humour chased a mangy cat from the spartan room that the Minke, myself and the Dutch would share for what was left of the night.

'I just need the bathroom,' the Minke said to me after we had had a much-needed hug, curtailed because we both felt gross covered in sweat, dust and road grime. 'Then bed. So I can straighten out.'

I smiled at her optimism as I checked out the beds, which were visibly banana-shaped. Turning down the unnecessary blanket on my bed I found a chicken's egg on my sheets.

'Ah! *Huevo! Que bueno!*' ('An egg! How good!') the hostel owner said in delight when I gave it to her, as if she'd won a prize, before walking out with it. I had to assume that the bed's previous occupant was a chicken, and the sheets hadn't been changed since then, but by then I was too tired to care.

Soon after, Lisa returned from the bathroom, looking shell-shocked. 'My God. I don't think that room has ever been cleaned. And the wall is so thin between it and this room I could almost see you.' I decided to use a tree outside instead, chasing a sleeping chicken from underneath in doing so. 'One of your kids was in my room,' I said to it as it scuttled off.

I fell deeply asleep, but was woken after what seemed like a very brief time by Cesar's bass voice shouting '*Vamos!*' before the rooster outside could crow.

After an extraordinary breakfast of steak, eggs, rice, lettuce, tomato and an instant coffee so dastardly that even my caffeine-craving system rejected it, we were on the road again.

'Only three hours,' said Cesar, smiling.

'Sure,' I thought.

It took another eight hours from breakfast to reach our destination, meaning that all up we'd spent over twenty-two hours stewing in our own juices in the four-wheel drive, not to mention experiencing the terror of impending death. So it was a huge relief to be at the water for our relaxing float downriver. Little were we to know that this was where the real adventure would begin.

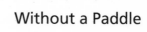

Despite our delayed arrival, our raft wasn't yet ready for launch from a river bank strewn with litter from a nearby village and landmined with dog turds. While the setting was less than idyllic, the river looked inviting. First though we had to meet our crew.

A hard-working man with a gold-toothed smile was lashing tyre tubes to a rectangular frame made of bamboo.

'Hmm, rubber, twine and bamboo, all noted shipbuilding materials,' I mused, watching him, though I quite liked the rough look of our vessel as it came together. How could this not be fun?

The gold-toothed man introduced himself as Abel, and introduced us to his wife, Reina, who would be our cook.

'*Mucho gusto*, Reina,' we all replied, Thema rolling the 'r' at the front of her name as if he found it delicious.

One further crew member sat watching us all toad-like through heavy-lidded eyes. Though it was evident he put in a lot of effort at the gym, he clearly didn't replicate it in the boat-building endeavour.

'Our son,' Abel explained, a hint of resignation in his tone. He offered no name, and a few of us quietly agreed to think of the lad as Captain Useless.

Thanks to Abel's heroic solo labour, in no time we were boarding, our luggage wrapped in two-ply plastic bags in case of splashes or, worse, a flip. The luggage then doubled as our seats and I quickly discovered that a bird book has nasty edges to sit on, and resolved to repack it more sensibly the next day.

We set off into a side channel as the sun sank, our goal a much more impressive-looking river only a few hundred metres away. The tyre-tube raft bucked a little where the waters met but Abel's efforts with a paddle soon had us in calmer waters, and before long a feeling of absolute serenity overtook us. Jesus was no longer with us, and that was surely a blessing. Everyone was silent, enjoying the peace, except Thema, who started singing a few notes of some song, then muttered and, tranquillity trashed, went silent again.

'We will camp in an hour,' Cesar said after two minutes/hours and we all burst out laughing at the idea that he had any idea when that was. Though he probably didn't know what we were laughing about, he joined in, and for the next two hours we happily let the current take us into the night, finally pulling in at an unnamed beach in a remote part of the world.

'This feels like South America, doesn't it?' I said to Lisa as we set up our camp for the night.

'Yes, it does,' she said, briefly letting go of a tent pole to squeeze my hand. 'But I'll admit I can't see anything here so we might be in London.'

•

Dawn revealed that we had set up camp on a flat mix of sand and river rocks (actually some of the rocks had made themselves known to my spine during the night). The river here was the colour and opacity of milky coffee.

On the opposite bank, some fifty metres or so away, men were already dredging and panning. Cesar explained that they were miners looking for gold. The miners set up a pump which emitted a dull thrumming, its outlet pipe spewing muddy waste straight back into the river, which explained the murky colour.

As we set off on the raft again I felt content. Every hope I had had for this trip was finally being fulfilled. The river was serene, even if the jungle on either side was disturbed by mining and the water often cloudy. The brochure hadn't mentioned that the herons, kingfishers, caimans and otters I'd hoped to see would be absent— there was no way they could hunt in this murk—yet the peacefulness made it impossible to be too disappointed.

Once more our little group from La Paz, never verbose, stayed quiet and simply enjoyed the view of the horizon-stretching river and its banks, the gentle lap of water against the raft (this led to the occasional buttock soaking, but no one complained) and the soft splish of Abel's paddle as he steered us down the centre of the river.

'Cesar,' I asked, 'what is the name of this river?'

'It is the Rio Kaka,' he replied.

It took a few moments for it to hit me. 'Shit Creek? That's fantastic!' I said, laughing, though nobody else seemed to share my delight in the waterway's name.

The day passed with little incident and few breaks, Cesar keen to make up the time lost by our late arrival by encouraging Abel and his loafing son to paddle while the rest of us sat, chatted, and tanned on the raft.

We set up camp again in the dark, the fire lit first so Reina could make us what turned out to be a surprisingly tasty meal given the deceptively plain ingredients of bread, tinned tuna and a mystery sauce, as well as plaintain, the savoury banana that is a staple in many South American countries.

The next morning we were woken by what had become the familiar Cesar alarm clock. 'Abel!' he would shout in his bass voice. '*Vamos!*'

By day three we saw fewer and fewer signs of people. The banks were no longer gouged by mining and the river ran cleaner, with increasing numbers of streams joining it from the surrounding low hills. Macaws flew overhead and branches shook with the weight of fleeing monkeys, their fear of humans a sign that they were most likely hunted in this area. Among the dense greenery was the odd orchid, a splash of yellow or red tended by bees the size of birds, and birds the size of bees.

On the fourth morning we were woken by something far louder than Cesar's bass rumble. A harsh, sustained bellow—changing in pitch but never waning—began before sunrise, rousing all but the dead from sleep.

'What the hell is that?' the Minke asked me.

'Howler monkeys. The world's loudest land animal,' I replied, grinning in the dark. I'd glimpsed them before in the Pantanal, but hadn't heard them calling properly until now, and only knew what the sound was because there was simply nothing else it could be.

The aptly named howler monkeys kept their chorus going all through our breakfast, then went silent as they headed off to find their own food.

By now, despite some sunburn and Thema's uncanny ability to wait until people had just begun to doze off before hitting us with a phrase of an unknown song, I was more relaxed than I had been in years. South America was teaching me that it wasn't just adventure I had given up to sit behind a desk. Feelings of peace and contentment had become so foreign to me during the last seven years in Sydney that at first I resisted them, in case I became accustomed to them and was heartbroken once they were taken away again. But the river won, and by the fourth day I was little more animated than a carrot, but surely much happier. Having Lisa to share it with made it even more special, and she whispered in my ear one night that she was glad we came on the trip, and even more that we'd been on the same bus all those months ago in Patagonia.

•

On the fifth day, though, everything changed. Somehow we had made up the lost time from our late arrival and Cesar promised that we would make it to our destination, the small jungle town of Rurrenabaque, by nightfall.

'Lah, lah, lah,' Thema responded flatly to the news.

'Oh, come on!' I protested. 'That's not even a song.'

Despite the pleasure we had all taken in the trip we now began fantasising about a shower, a bed that didn't deflate during the night, beer, and fatty food like pizza (Reina's impressive earlier fare had dried up and our more recent meals had been variations on fried plantain—which, without condiments, we discovered to be as tasty as an old sponge).

The scenery, which had been subtly changing since our trip began, gave way dramatically, with sheer cliffs soaring on either side of us, their sides worn smooth from years of the river's work. By now the water was clear, and at last I saw some herons, standing on rounded ledges, staring intently at the river, waiting to spear any fish that ventured too close to them.

Then just as suddenly we emerged from the canyon, and the river fanned out to the greatest width we had seen so far, perhaps two hundred metres across. The currents and countercurrents this change set up made the surface a sequin-dazzle of ripples, and our little raft jolted as if being dragged over cobbles.

A sideways thrust suddenly caught us and despite hard paddling from Abel and some desultory stirs at the back from his son, the raft was dragged close to the bank. A visible current ran against the river's flow, and a line as definite as lane markings on a highway showed where the two currents met each other. The circular span of spinning water covered almost the whole width of the river, and there was no way of avoiding it. Soon we were heading back upriver, until the current we were trapped in pushed against the rocks and shot us back in the direction of Rurrenabaque. Yet this was no cause for celebration, because we were heading towards far more turbulent water. My heart thumped as I realised we were going to be sucked into the dangerous-looking whirlpool ahead of us.

The front left corner of the raft dipped down as we hit the swirl, water rushing up and over Abel, then onto the Minke, myself and English Nick. Bucking and bobbing, the raft spun round in a sickening circle. Despite being drenched, Abel kept his rowing regular and strong. As we spun faster and deeper into the whirlpool I clutched at my smaller backpack like it was my baby. My larger backpack could be sacrificed but this one contained all my most treasured possessions—a camera, my binoculars and bird books.

The whirlpool abruptly spat us out, soaking everyone at the back, then the raft was caught once more in the cross-current and we shot back in the direction we'd come. Again, Abel leant hard into his strokes. Glancing back I saw Captain Useless dipping his paddle as though he were stirring tea and didn't want it to slosh out of his cup.

The whirlpool had an inexorable pull, and after one lap past the bank we were sucked straight back into the centre, sinking deeper, the water coming up to my waist and grabbing me like desperate hands, pulling and tugging.

'Hold on,' I shouted, as much to myself as anyone else, as we spun deeper into a chaos of foam and turgid water. The stoic Abel kept paddling, somehow not flung from the raft despite having no handhold.

A sudden savage lurch saw the paddle ripped from Abel's grasp and accelerate past us into the spiral of water. I looked back at Abel's son, who was similarly empty-handed, his paddle also ripped away, or perhaps thrown away for fear of having to use it.

'Without a paddle!' I shouted, laughing hysterically despite the danger we were in. The whole raft angled sideways now, leaning into the vortex, and while it wasn't quite a science-fiction waterspout with a huge cavity that could swallow us whole, I did imagine that when we hit its middle we'd all be sent flying; in that sort of water even the Minke with her fins for feet might struggle.

The rear of the raft dipped, touched the middle; we spun, and somehow crested out of the turbulence, back into the mad looping current again. We could maybe paddle for the bank, using our arms and whatever tools we had, then portage the raft until we were past the vortex, but Abel and Cesar gave no orders.

'A paddle!' the Dutchman shouted, and we turned to see it bob to the surface, tantalisingly close. 'I'll get it,' he added, making as if to dive in.

'No! You'll die,' shouted the Minke, causing his girlfriend to clasp a vice-like hand on his arm.

Attached to the raft by twine was a loose tube which we'd used as a dinghy of sorts when someone wanted off the main vessel. The Minke offered to get into it and scull her way to the errant oar, but Abel had a better idea, and reeled the tube towards himself, then threw it like a life ring, snaring the paddle and drawing it in.

At the same time we were heading back into the whirlpool. Abel leant deeper into his strokes, and those on the same side as him used their hands and even a book to paddle along with him. The sucking noise of the whirlpool grew louder, and we drew closer, angling in despite the grunts of effort aboard; then the front of the raft nudged the edge of the maelstrom, but this time it did not dip, and instead we sailed past, the circle broken, on the way to Rurrenabaque.

'My God, did we almost die then?' came the voice of someone from the back.

'Yep,' I answered, still looking resolutely ahead, still holding the raft so tightly it's amazing I didn't pop a tyre tube. A pulse thrummed in my ear and I knew that I was grinning, feeling a thrill usually reserved for some wildlife encounter. 'Makes you feel alive though, doesn't it?'

'Loony,' said the Minke, leaning over to peck my cheek.

'Oh yes,' I thought, 'loony for sure, but alive. Alive!'

Drunk with relief we laughed through the last leg, cheering the sun on as it sank and threatened to break Cesar's promise of arrival by sundown, then erupting into cheers when the town came into sight as the barest solar sliver hovered over the river's surface.

'Nicely done, Cesar, nicely done,' I said, still buoyant in the adrenal afterglow, and not even minding when, to celebrate our arrival, Thema burst into song.

One Hundred Ways to Bleed

After our miraculously punctual arrival in the small jungle town of Rurrenabaque, we spent two days luxuriating in warmish showers and well-stocked bars. Our next adventure—again a watery one—would set off three hours down yet another rattling South American road.

Old hands now, I turned to Lisa as we departed another cramped minivan, with a different group of travellers this time, and asked, 'Are my teeth loose?'

'Which ones?'

'All of them.' I grinned maniacally.

Unlike the epic rafting trip with Abel and Captain Useless, this river journey would offer situations literally more hairy, as this was a wildlife-rich area. Many tour operators used the same point as an embarkation area, and almost one hundred people were milling around, waiting to be allocated a canoe and guide. The cluster the Minke and I had joined was a mixed bag of a pair of my fellow Australians, an English couple and two French travellers, who were either mute or had no interest in speaking to us, Eric, our guide, or each other. I'd only figured their nationality based on the names they'd given when I introduced myself.

•

Despite being landlocked, Bolivia maintains a navy, a relic from the days before they lost coastal access in a war with Chile. We watched and waited while a Bolivian official, spruce in his uniform, made sure that the flotilla of motorised canoes we'd be travelling in for the next stage of our journey were counted and ticked off. He did so with all the professionalism that fully loaded battleships would require, frowning as he double-counted every vessel. As the little group that would join the Minke and me waited to be told to board, our guide, Eric, stood watching with a broad smile that we were soon to realise was semi-permanent.

Eventually there were only a few canoes left. 'All those ones,' said Eric, waving towards the river as the last few canoes disappeared, 'will go too fast, and make too much noise. We'll go slowly and quietly, and see lots of animals!'

'Oh, I like this,' I thought. So with smiling Eric in the rear, our small group set off last, saluting the naval officer, who just glared back at us, maybe imagining a vast ocean he might one day command, or perhaps just lay his eyes on.

Unlike the jungle we'd got used to seeing on our raft trip, this time we were surrounded by sprawling pampas on either side. Pampas areas are tropical, but with far more expanses of open grassland than jungle. And while this habitat lacks the kaleidoscopic biodiversity of the rainforests, we were likely to see more animals because the open pampas allows viewers to see that much further, and animals that live there are more accustomed to being watched by humans and are thus less inclined to run away.

A few trees sprang up from the plains, and in places the river banks were overrun with scrambled shrubs and liana vines in which monkeys clambered. Often the monkeys would beg for fruit from people in the passing boats, behaviour resulting from bad tourism practices, and I was glad to see that grinning Eric didn't encourage such activities.

As Eric steered us along the river's wending course, smiling at his surrounds, giggling at the monkeys and occasionally pointing out the caimans sunning themselves on the bank, my hopes rose that this was the right sort of place to see a jaguar.

'Oh my goodness!' Eric exclaimed, the phrase sounding quaint in his accented English. 'I've never seen that before!'

I swivelled around, trying to see what he was referring to. Nearby, a flicker of movement became a ripple, and I realised that what I was looking at was a caiman that had caught a snake. But not just any snake. It was an anaconda.

'Wow! Take some photos, please. The other guides won't believe me!' said Eric, laughing, as if their doubt was the funniest thing imaginable. Quite thrilled, we carried on. I felt my luck curve take an upswing and wondered if maybe, just maybe, we might see something very special here. Something with spots.

Not long after our sighting of the anaconda-eating caiman, a certain smell began to tickle my nose which I recognised as the distinctive odour of marijuana. Puttering around a corner we caught sight of another canoe, moving even more slowly than ours, puffs of grey-white smoke emanating from it, and not from the motor.

The guide for the magic dragon group stood at the back, wearing a khaki camouflage shirt with torn-off sleeves, a knife of ridiculous proportions hanging from his belt. I've never been to a wilderness area that didn't have guides like him, the sort that take the job not because they love animals or the outdoors, but because they think it makes them look tough and will impress girls. At the front of

El Macho's canoe stood one of the tourists, heavily muscled, with a military-looking close crop of hair.

In countries with tourism industries, the least-popular tourists will often be those who visit in the greatest numbers. Thus, in parts of Africa, Americans are unloved; in Mozambique, South Africans are often reviled; the Brits have a reputation in southern Spain. But in Bolivia the dominant and most disliked tourists are Israelis, and this canoe clearly held a group of Israelis doing their bit to further damage the reputation of their country.

I didn't care where they were from, or that they were smoking weed, or even that they were making more noise than is appropriate in a wilderness area, but my hackles rose as I saw the muscle-bound tourist reach down into the canoe and come up with a stick which he threw at a caiman that was sunning itself on the bank. Even though the stick was little more than a twig, and it missed, and even if it had hit the caiman's armoured skin could easily take such a blow, a cold fury began to course in my veins as it does whenever I witness any sort of cruelty to animals.

My icy rage grew as he reached back down and then threw another stick, missing again, but this time sending the caiman scuttling into the water. For a while we lost sight of him as his canoe rounded a bend but then saw him again throwing sticks at caimans. Mutters of 'what a wanker' rose from our canoe.

'He'll run out of sticks,' I thought, steam all but whistling from my ears. Sure enough, he was soon out of ammo. But the guide then did one of the worst things I've ever seen a guide do, pulling over so Muscles could gather more sticks. Apoplectic with rage by now, I was ready to dive into the water and try to overtake their canoe with furious paddling, haul the muscly guy out of the boat, and then . . . well, I had no plan, but something that would hurt him before he drowned me. But the Minke made soothing noises at me and maybe even physically restrained me.

Now Muscles started throwing sticks at anything in sight, including a heron that had its back to him yet somehow detected the missile in the last fraction of a second and flared its wings, sidestepping the stick he'd thrown. Birds not only lack the caiman's armour, but have bones light and hollow for flight, and even a small blow can break their limbs. The bird would have died had it been hit, possibly not immediately but over some days as it weakened.

By now I hated not just the stick thrower, but the guide. 'Why doesn't he stop him?' I asked Eric, just to say something and unclench my jaw.

For once Eric was not smiling; he simply said, 'That guide is not a good one.'

I was also furious with Muscles' group. Surely there was someone aboard who could see that what he was doing was wrong? Maybe he was such an alpha male that the men were cowed, but one of the women could have humbled him. Yet no one did anything; they just puffed away at their joints and laughed at every missile he threw.

Finally they slowed, and nudged into a bank near a campsite festooned with the word '*Flecha*', Spanish for arrow. It wasn't planned, but as we puttered within range I stood up abruptly, causing a slight sway in the canoe that Eric was forced to correct, taking us a little closer to the alighting group.

'Hey! Digestive exit!' I shouted, or words that described such a thing in cruder terms.

Not surprisingly, they all turned to look at me.

'No, you! Genital skull!' I shouted (or words to that effect), waggling an outstretched finger at the muscled man as I called him after many unmentionable forms of waste, as well as accusing him of taking great pleasure in activities with his family that were not only distasteful but, frankly, impossible without surgery.

Muscles just stood there looking in perplexity at the frenzied little man shouting at him; finally it dawned on me that he genuinely didn't know what he'd done to earn this diatribe. Eric sensibly had not slowed nor deviated in his course, clearly not wanting to be part of any intergroup brawl, and I was now swivelled at the waist shouting back at Muscles. I tried to think of a strong finish, but could only come up with, 'Don't throw sticks!' Then, after a brief pause, I added, 'At animals!'

And they were gone. I sat down, feeling a tad foolish, shaking with the adrenalin that any sort of conflict produces. Loud applause followed, and the sound of many birds taking flight, and I realised my group was clapping me.

As my fury waned and the ice left my veins I began to wonder about the origins of the tattoo I'd seen on Muscles' shoulder. It was likely, I realised, that we'd run into his group again over the next few days. Maybe he was special forces, I thought. Or a ninja.

I was dead, I just didn't smell like it yet.

•

We arrived at our camp that evening to discover it was a shared one, and among the group already there found David/Adair from the rafting trip. I genuinely liked David so it was great to see him. After a quick catch-up the conversation turned to the antics of his countrymen that afternoon, with the Minke describing the stick thrower's behaviour.

He was very embarrassed, and explained, 'He's probably straight out of the military. They come here because it's a cheap place to visit, but they're just looking to let off steam and probably have no real interest in where they are.'

'Don't worry, one day I'll meet you in Bali and then I can be embarrassed by Australians,' I said; then, still curious, I described the shape and positioning of Muscles' tattoo.

'Hmm, really?' said David. 'Ex-commando.'

'So not a ninja, then. Thank goodness,' I said.

'He's the sort of guy who knows a hundred ways to make you bleed.'

'Excellent. Thanks,' I said.

'Pretty brutal what they do,' said David. 'Hopefully you won't run into him again.'

'I'm sure I'll be fine,' I said, and though I didn't really believe what I was saying, I still didn't regret what I'd done.

'Okay. Just be careful though. Those guys aren't known to be forgiving.'

'Please feel free not to tell me any more.'

Unfortunately, David's comments had piqued the interest of the rest of the group, and over dinner that night the conversation largely centred on the highly trained ex-commando I'd berated earlier that day. I pretended to be unconcerned but privately started to imagine a number of different scenarios, most of them including an ambush and significant loss of blood on my part.

The mere thought of conflict usually makes my eyes water, and I'd long believed there was no finer form of self-defence than absence (I also put a lot of faith in my one athletic gift—I am a very fast runner). But revelation came in the form of a quote from Winston

Churchill, who'd once said, 'I do not trust a man without enemies. It means he has never stood up for anything.' I believed in the stance I had taken on the boat, and did not mind having an enemy. I just wished it was one I was more likely to defeat in combat.

'I have a plan. I'm going to blame Aaron,' I said to the Minke, pointing at the largest member of our group, a heavily built Australian with broad shoulders and an imposing beard.

'Won't work,' said the Minke laconically. 'The commando saw your mouth moving. And your hands flapping around.'

'Aha!' I exclaimed. 'I'll just have to say he's a ventriloquist and had his hand up my bum.'

'You really have no shame, do you?' the Minke said with more resignation than dismay.

•

The very next day we saw the magic dragon group trudging through a swampy section of the pampas, no doubt in search of anacondas. A few minutes later their guide, still in his macho vest, held one up above his head with a roar of triumph.

Before we'd set out, Eric had cautioned us against picking up any anacondas we saw: some of them were big enough to eat us, he explained, but it was also impossible to know what sort of stress it caused them. Most of us were wearing insect repellent, which might harm them if it was transferred to them. Now, at the sight of the snake being manhandled, the usually smiling Eric stormed over and delivered a rapid-fire mouthful of invective at the other guide, who had draped the anaconda around the neck of one member of his group. Despite his unimpressive physical presence, Eric's tone had sufficient authority that the snake was quickly released and Macho's group moved on. Luckily, the ex-commando didn't see me standing behind the Minke.

•

On the final day of our tour, without having had a whiff of jaguar, we set out before dawn to do some wildlife watching before the nocturnal animals settled down for the day. Eric guided our canoe to a high bank of the river, which we scrambled up to be rewarded with a view of the surrounding flatlands and the wobbling sun as it rose. It was so serene that for the first time since I'd seen sticks being thrown at animals I forgot about commandos, stopped hearing the nagging voice reminding me I had not seen a jaguar, and exhaled.

My reverie was soon broken by the revving of a motor, and another canoe soon arrived at what I already thought of territorially as our spot.

'Oh goody,' I thought, seeing the distinct military haircut at the bow. At least he wasn't standing up. At least he wasn't holding sticks. It surprised me that his group had managed such an early start, as their focus in our brief meetings had seemed to be on partying, not wildlife, but they now moved with some urgency up the bank to catch the last of the sunrise—a futile measure, as close to the equator the sun ejects from the horizon like bread from a toaster.

As their group formed up, maintaining a distinct divide from us in the way humans do when two herds meet, I kept my eyes firmly on the commando, ready to break eye contact (and probably wind) if he looked at me. He stood aggressively, shoulders bunched as if ready to swing into violent action; it was the pose of an alpha gorilla unlikely to let an insult pass. Usually I aim to defuse tension with humour, but in this case there could be a language barrier, so in the

event of conflict my only chance, I decided, was to make a dive for
the river and rely on the slim hope that commandos couldn't swim.

One of his group broke away and headed into some waist-high
grass behind us, a wheaty expanse for many hundred metres. As he
moved, the commando looked my way with a scowl. I turned and
braced myself to take a running dive.

From behind us came the rasp of a zip, clear in the still morning
air, and I waited for the gush of urine that the departed Israeli was
surely going to unleash (at what I thought was an impolite proximity
to the gathering). Instead there was a girlish squeal, the thunder of
feet and a guttural Hebrew curse.

Both groups had been facing the now-risen sun, watching its
reflection redden the water, but we all swivelled en masse at the
disturbance. The erstwhile urinator had woken a sleeping capybara
that was now desperate to avoid being peed on, or was perhaps
furious at the indignity of it all, and was doing what capybara do
when threatened, and heading for the water. Unfortunately our group
was in its way.

Capybaras are far from sluggish and this one was coming at us
at ramming speed. Weighing up to forty-five kilos, a capybara bowling
you over could cause serious injury, and I really wished that I knew
how to handle this species like I did those in Africa. Should you
stand your ground or run? Or throw a commando at it and let them
sort it out? But there was no time to put that plan in place. Several
of us sidestepped, some throwing themselves bodily out of harm's
way as the rodent charged through the gap we'd made then scampered
down the bank and plunged into the river, its splash exposing a
jagged stump that would have impaled me had I made my own
planned exit.

Both groups re-formed like schooling fish, but this time with no gap between us, united by the experience. Most people were laughing, a common response to shock, led by Eric who was delighted by the encounter. I was chuckling away too, but warily eyed the commando for a few tense seconds before Eric said it was too crowded and we should move on.

I waited for a voice to call me back or a sucker punch to the back of my head, but we returned to our canoe without incident. This made me wonder if the commando had considered his sins and felt some shame, or whether he was mellower than I had given him credit for, or merely dulled by dope.

While I accepted that diplomacy might be the better approach in future, all I knew was that I had stood up for something that mattered to me. I probably hadn't taught him anything—in fact, he undoubtedly respected my stand as much as a pigeon respects a statue. Nevertheless, I felt a small sense of pride from the experience, even if it had taken an oversized guinea pig to save me.

The Idiot Box

Over the years I'd been approached several times by producers who'd read my books about safari guiding in Africa and who were interested in making a TV show based on them. While these opportunities had all dried up, I received a new approach while I was travelling in South America which felt different, like we might make something worthwhile, in contrast to the current crop of wildlife shows which all seemed to involve the host diving onto animals then proclaiming, 'He seems a bit agitated,' as the creature struggles to get free. Despite myself, I started getting excited that we could make a show that was based on information and conservation.

Back in Australia the occasional day's test filming had led to adventures like being locked in a cage with white lions—a welcome escape from my office routine and a reminder of what I was passionate about. Though the concept of being on television caused some mixed feelings, since I cherish the relative anonymity of being an author, there were some good reasons to be enthusiastic this time. The production company told me that one of their priorities was highlighting issues of conservation. If it worked out, presenting a TV show would also fulfil my desire to continue travelling the world watching animals, and would pay far better than writing alone.

After our boating adventures, the Minke and I had decided to travel further north, and when the production company wanted to do a test shoot we agreed that the best place to meet was Colombia.

'Is it really safe here?' Michael asked. He would be producer, director and cameraman for the shoot, and had just landed at Bogotá airport. He was referring to the country's violent reputation as a hotbed for criminal activities run by drug lords. Lisa and I had already spent two weeks travelling through some of its towns and coffee-growing regions and had found them nothing but charming.

'Seems it,' I replied, and that was true as far as our experiences went.

Lisa didn't care to accompany us for the test shoot, and went head alone to Cartagena, a Spanish colonial city on the Caribbean coast, where I intended to join her three days later. I wasn't perturbed at the thought of her travelling alone because of how safe the country felt, and because she was more than savvy enough to go alone—in fact had done so for several months before we had met. Also, I would back her in a bar fight any day.

'It seems very safe,' I reassured Michael, who still seemed nervous.

He might have had a point. I'd arranged a naturalist guide to accompany us, but we were heading into more remote parts of the country, and there might still be rebel activity in these areas. And as well as the guerrilla groups, over the next two days of travel there was a chance we'd encounter pumas, bears, snakes and maybe, just maybe, a jaguar.

On the first day of travelling together, Michael and I were met in front of our hotel at the foul hour of four am by our guide, Diana, and a man named Eduardo who would act as our driver. From the look of his shaved head and bulging muscles he was likely to be talented at security too. His car was tiny, its tyres no larger than dinner plates. He squeezed his massive frame behind the wheel with difficulty, and drove with an arm out the window by necessity as much as attitude.

Bogotá is the world's second-highest capital city (after La Paz in Bolivia), but Eduardo drove us higher still, up and up. We passed panting cyclists struggling in the thin air, and I found the mere idea of exertion in this oxygen-depleted part of the world tiring.

After several hours' drive, and a break to partake of a local energy brew that consisted of hot water, huge chunks of palm sugar and a slab of rubbery white cheese, we reached Chingaza National Park, accessible only by special permission. The power a TV camera can wield became apparent, as the guards checking our papers were more interested in whether we were famous than if everything was in order.

After completing security we drove through gates into a place of clear streams and tussock grasses, as well as alien-looking plants with hairy leaves on dead-straight stems. Everything glistened with dew and our breath fogged with each exhalation. This habitat, called páramo, consisted of high-altitude wetland that was home to rarely seen species such as the mountain tapir, as well as more cosmopolitan animals like pumas and the continent-spanning white-tailed deer.

'More energy!' Michael called as I was doing my first piece to camera.

Whenever animals are the subject of general conversation I become very animated, and could flap my jaw at the person I'm talking to until their ears bleed. But talking to a camera is very different; addressing the lidless eye of the lens and the slow-blinking red light above I found it hard to muster anything more than a dull monotone.

'Páramo,' I said blandly, 'is high. Cold. Wet.'

'More energy!' Michael called again.

I remembered all the wildlife television hosts I'd seen over the years, bounding over rocks like mountain goats, jumping on animals, going into raptures at any critter they encountered. To show that I wasn't beyond such lunacy myself, I came up with the idea of sampling a plant, unwise given that my knowledge of local botany was negligible. Maybe, though, some plant compound could give me the manic energy I needed to cut it on film. I skipped the unappealing hairy plant and spied something that looked a little like rosemary. My taste test revealed it to be something you'd never add to a meal. As I spat out the bitter pith, Michael said, 'Great! Let's get some more of that!'

Diana directed Eduardo to drive us to likely habitats for pumas and other species, while Michael encouraged me to shout and gesticulate wildly for the camera, making so much noise that any sensible cat would emigrate in protest.

'Look at this!' I yelled, pointing at a pile of bones I'd found after climbing onto a small ledge.

Michael followed, slipping and sliding on the mossy rocks as he continued filming. I have long ago given up the idea of athletic prowess or even sure-footedness, and consider any day that I don't fall over or walk into anything a victory, but Michael was so out of his element in the wilderness that I felt like a ballerina. Gasping for breath, he joined me.

'Puma kill!' I said, genuinely excited now. Attached to the bones were some withered strips of sinew, skin turning to leather and a foot. 'See this! Not a hoof . . . looks like it was a fox!' I enjoy playing wildlife detective so I was grinning in genuine delight as I checked the carcass's surrounds and located the distinct pugmarks of a puma, still familiar from my time with Roy. 'Yes! Definitely a puma kill—not so fresh, maybe even a week or more old, but the overhang has protected the tracks from rain. Nice!'

'Hey,' Michael said, 'that was excellent. But you can hear my breathing on the tape. Can you do it again, with a bit more energy?'

•

Over dinner that night, back at our hotel, Michael revealed that this was his first wildlife shoot, his usual work being studio based. It turned out he had shot several feature films I'd seen and enjoyed. Movies are a side passion of mine and we stayed up talking later than we should have given that another brutally early start was scheduled for the next day.

When I expressed concern at being tired for the next day's filming, Michael assured me that if I could be as animated as I'd just been during our conversation we'd be able to nail it.

But there was no nailing. With no emotional feedback from the lens I came across as cold and emotionless as a toilet bowl, but nowhere near as deep. On day two we travelled to the lowlands, a place of tangled trees and busy streams, chattering with birds and monkeys. There might be jaguars here, but Michael, keen to get a worthy performance from me, kept calling for more energy, and by energy he meant shouty enthusiasm. If all the noise I made didn't drive away the wildlife then the strange rictus I wore to show enthusiasm just might. Watching the playback I saw someone who looked like me but with a leery grin that would make sensible people lock up their daughters—and maybe bring Grandma in off the porch too.

Only when Michael took long shots of me seeing patches of the jungle for the first time did he capture my genuine love for all wild places, but the interspersed pieces to camera spoiled any useful footage he had.

The last segment was to be shot in a cave, which excited me because according to Diana it held five species of bats, including one with long fangs that drink blood. Vampires. I'd never seen them, and was keen for a close look.

'Don't forget, you need to project lots of energy!' said Michael as we headed into the cave. Already that day I had climbed trees and a rock face to demonstrate that I was not a zombie, and while I did appreciate the opportunity being offered to me, suddenly the whole idea of appearing on screen was wearisome.

Yet real energy came to me when I met my first vampire bat. I'd read up on them in anticipation of this trip and knew they were unlikely to be dangerous—less than half of one per cent of bats carry rabies. (In fact, non-blood-sucking bats are more dangerous than vampires because their dung can harbour a fungus that causes a deadly lung disease.) Rising to my full height in the cave I came eye to eye with a roosting vampire and smiled in delight. My teeth are one of my more prominent features, and smiling at animals is generally a bad thing because showing your teeth suggests you are about to use them. The other bat species in the cave had taken off before I could get close, but the vampires all flashed their fangs straight back at my unintentional threat.

Unlike the other bats, vampires are able to run on the ground, an adaptation for their blood-sucking lifestyle. From the air they locate warm-blooded prey, such as a cow or even a sleeping human, land nearby, then walk towards it on their back legs and elbows before making incisions with their razor-sharp teeth and lapping at the flow of blood (unlike the creature of myth they are named after, they don't suck blood—merely lick it). As they drink, their saliva mingles with the blood, releasing an enzyme with the truly wonderful name of draculin. This stops blood clotting, so the wound continues to bleed long after the bat has had its tablespoon or so of dinner.

While I had learnt all the above from my reading, I didn't know that vampires can run while upside down, so when one abandoned its toothy threat display and scurried along the cave roof towards my face I was taken aback.

'Hey!' I said sharply, as if dealing with a cantankerous lion (and forgetting that this bat probably only understood Spanish). I'd always been taught not to run away from large animals, and had held my ground against lions, elephants, leopards and the like, but I instinctively took a step back from the bat, stones clattering at my heels, the sound reverberating in the cave. Loud enough to a human, the sound I'd made was possibly deafening to the four other bat species, who hunt using echolocation. They took off, several thousands of wings beating in the air and swirling around, the bats wanting to escape the noise without leaving the cave and facing the light. Despite this, they were so adept at using sonar not one collided with me in the maelstrom. The vampires, perturbed by the activity, joined the other species in the air.

Michael gave a not quite manly squeal as one of the vampires dive-bombed him, flying straight at the lens. Later he showed me the playback; while admittedly a bat approaching at speed is far more threatening in the widescreen he viewed it in, at the time his undignified exit from the cave was merely entertaining. He was okay, though, so I suggested we get back to work while I was still showing signs of life.

Re-entering the cave I heard Michael stumbling behind me. I understood it was difficult to simultaneously look through the camera and cover uneven terrain, and I had earlier kicked the stones myself, so I wasn't frustrated until he said, 'More energy, but move slowly!'

'How?' I said. The whole thing suddenly seemed so ludicrous that I burst out laughing. A startled bat devised a fitting punishment, lightening his load by relieving himself copiously onto my shirt.

For some reason I have always found the idea of monkeys defecating in their hands and throwing it at observers (not uncommon behaviour in zoos) wildly amusing, and even nicknamed one of my friends 'Poo-monkey', so perhaps what I'd received was a deserved double payback. However, monkeys eat fruit and bugs, which make disgusting enough droppings, but a diet of only blood makes for even nastier excrescences.

'Oh man, that stinks!' Michael said.

'I'm just glad it wasn't Robert Pattinson,' I replied.

'Hey man, that's funny, say it again!' said Michael, swinging the camera towards me.

Unfortunately, once more the moment was lost and my delivery was flat.

As the months went by, fewer and fewer emails came in from the company, and I knew that they would move on to other potential projects. I wasn't offended and knew much of the blame lay with me.

Among what small disappointment I felt about it there was a nugget of delight. In the past I'd experienced failure by being a fool, but with television at last I'd found a field where I didn't cut it because I wasn't a big enough idiot.

Beekeeping in the Amazon

'Honey, what did he say?' the woman asked her husband loudly, even though the man she was referring to was standing right beside her and understood English.

'He said it was to the left of the tree,' her husband replied, not very helpfully as we were in the rainforest and trees were pretty plentiful.

'Oh,' she said, apparently satisfied. Then, mouth agape, she raised binoculars to her eyes and began a hectic scan—up, down, left, right and back—but the bird she was trying to see evaded her.

'Darn it, where has it gone?' she asked, though the bird hadn't moved.

'To the left of the tree,' I said mischievously, able to do so because I wasn't guiding this group—hadn't been a guide for ten years in fact.

A man named Oscar was in charge of our group, and he'd been in the guide business for twenty straight years. The downturned lines set firmly into his face suggested he only smiled when paid to do so. I felt for him. There was nothing monumentally wrong with this group. They weren't unpleasant. They weren't overly demanding. They were just really irritating. Maybe I was prone to irritation because after eight months together Lisa had headed back to London, her year's leave over, and I would not see her for another two months. In November I would visit her in the UK before carrying on with my South American journey.

'Don't do anything I wouldn't do!' she'd shouted as she departed from Bogotá airport.

'I'm going to do heaps of things you wouldn't!' I replied, mock perplexed. 'Like pee standing up!' The last sight I had of her was her shaking head, and not for the first time I wondered what she saw in me.

•

Oscar, the guide, bore the onerous responsibility of ensuring everyone enjoyed their stay at the beautiful Sacha Lodge, a property on the banks of the Napo River in the Ecuadorian Amazon. This patch of forest—an island of jungle surrounded by oilfields and logging interests—was only maintained thanks to tourist dollars, so keeping people happy was not just Oscar's job, but a deeply important responsibility.

This was the first time since arriving in South America that I had real work to do, but what lovely work it was! The owners of the lodge had been on safari in Africa and were impressed by African guiding standards. They'd asked me to spend a month at Sacha and let them know what I felt could be done better. I was grateful to be doing them this favour because the property was not only beautiful but fascinating, aswarm with different species of monkey and birds; it also contained two amazing structures that allowed you to climb above the forest canopy and look at animals that rarely or never descended, such as sloths and howler monkeys.

At the same time I felt a bit uncomfortable about my role at Sacha: all the guides I'd been out with were very impressive and professional, but though I'd told them that I'd worked as a guide myself, none of them knew I was there to assess for their boss.

'I realised today that working with tourists is like working with bees,' I said later that afternoon to Dan, one of the guides who'd shown me around before I joined Oscar's group.

'How so?' he asked, looking through a book of the region's snakes to try to identify a species he'd seen earlier.

'Most days are fine—you enjoy your job, maybe even love it,' I explained. 'But then one day you get a prick. And then after more good days you get another prick. And another. You can handle these, but over time the pricks accumulate, until finally your system can't take it anymore and one day you discover that you're allergic. And once you're allergic you can never work with bees again.'

'Okay,' said Dan, clearly unimpressed by my analogy.

I wandered off, still pondering my bee-sting epiphany.

The irritating people in his group were not just a problem for Oscar, they were upsetting me too; an idea had been brewing in my mind as I travelled through South America, and now, due to my bee-sting realisation, that idea was deflating at pace, making a raspberry noise as it zipped and withered and flew out the window. I was well aware my travelling days would eventually come to an end, and at some point I'd need to start earning money again. But I simply could not return to Sydney and plug away at a job I cared nothing for with the sole aim of getting ahead in life.

It was clear by now that the TV production company wasn't going to call back, and guiding was the only job I really felt qualified for. Sharing my passion for animals and the wilderness was perhaps the only work I was ever good at. Before arriving in Sacha I'd thought that maybe, just maybe, I would fall in love with the place, and be invited to come out of my long retirement from guiding and take a job there. However, as Oscar led us on another walk in search of the region's astonishing diversity of birds I began to fear I had become permanently allergic to tourists. It wasn't anything to do with Oscar, who was a great guide with sharp eyes and an encyclopaedic knowledge of bird calls. We ticked off species with the sort of names that make non-bird watchers roll their eyes—rufous-capped antthrush, white-browed wood-wren, short-billed foliage-gleaner and the quite lovely blue-crowned motmot. But my enjoyment of the sightings was tempered by my allergy to the woman who kept insisting she couldn't see, or hear, what we were looking at or for. It had occurred to me at one stage that she might be partially deaf, or blind, and I briefly felt like a thorough bastard for holding her in contempt. But then her husband spoke to her in a low whisper which she obviously understood perfectly, so I went back to being irritated.

Adding to my sense of frustration, I still hadn't spotted a jaguar; I was told that while they might occasionally pass through Sacha, none of the guides had ever seen one on the property, and the closest I'd come was some big-cat tracks Dan had told me about that tourists had trampled over before I could look at them. But in all honesty it wasn't the jaguar I was missing, really. It was more that I hadn't found a life worth living. I'd hoped that South America would inspire me in the same way Africa had, and that I would find a place there that I could settle into for a while before the urge to travel overtook me again. So far, however, there'd always been a reason to move on. And while I'd follow Lisa almost anywhere, I knew that her base of London was somewhere I would stagnate just as fast as Sydney. Homelessness didn't bother me as a rule, but I wanted at least the option of somewhere I could retreat to happily if need be.

My musings were interrupted by Oscar calling, 'Look! Leftie the light!' in his broken English and directing his laser pointer off the trail with great excitement. I spun around in time to see a monkey pop into view. It was cat-sized, and entirely black except for a cute white patch around its mouth and nose from which it took its Spanish name of *beber leche* (which means 'drink milk'). More monkeys followed and soon the whole troop was crossing overhead, using branches as trampolines, their athleticism so impressive it almost felt as though they were showing off for our benefit.

'Wow! Monkeys!' the woman exclaimed loudly, and stood there slack-jawed, head back, watching their passage. With an uncanny similarity to my experience in the bat cave, the woman's booming voice gave one monkey a big fright, and its bowels loosened in fear.

If there was a God as vindictive as me the resulting mess might have landed in the woman's mouth, but instead it only splattered her backpack. And despite the immediate rotten-fruit bouquet emanating from behind her she didn't notice this either—or my mirth as I covertly chuckled away.

'Nice shot, monkey,' I whispered. However juvenile my pleasure, I was suddenly brimming with happiness, and I let go of my earlier worries. This was not Africa, I reminded myself, and to compare it to Africa was as foolish as measuring it against Paris. And to dislike this woman just for her rudeness to guides and general asininity was unfair and reflected far more poorly on me than it did on her. Perhaps I was so disdainful because I was afraid that if I didn't find a worthy way to spend my life I might become like her. It was time to take all the joy I could from South America, to enjoy it whether or not I wanted to stay there long term, and live and laugh as much as possible in the extraordinary places I was lucky enough to visit.

(And yet, a small voice nagged, it would have been even better if the monkey poo had landed in her mouth, right?)

•

And there was much to like about life as I lazed around in between activities at Sacha Lodge. Every day I was coming across new species of all forms of life, from anteaters to electric eels, and eating bounteously. In fact, my daily walks were proving no match for the amount I was eating, so I decided I should take advantage of the lagoon in front of the lodge and get some exercise more strenuous than mastication.

Shaped like a half-moon, the lagoon stretched perhaps a kilometre either side of the lodge's deck, its dark waters meeting the shore roughly two hundred metres opposite. A small grassy area on the far bank—cut occasionally by channels that drained the surrounding swamps and gave the lagoon its dark tea colour—gave way to tall trees alive with monkeys and birds.

When I first saw the lodge I was surprised at its position by the lagoon, thinking it would be heaven for mosquitoes but hell for anyone with blood in their veins and skin to be punctured. However, Dan explained that the water from the swamps was rich in tannins leached from decaying leaves, and was thus too acidic for mosquitoes to lay their eggs in. As a result, the deck overlooking the lagoon was unspoiled.

Following my resolution to take up swimming, I stood in my swimmers on said deck eyeing the diving board mounted at its edge. Raised a mere two metres above the water's surface, it was still high enough to trigger my fear of heights, and I started making excuses to myself not to use it, which were quickly countered by the voice of rationality. What if a stump was hidden underneath the water? (They had all been cleared long ago, doofus.) What if an enormous caiman had just moved in? (No enormous caimans have been seen here for years, you wimp.) What if I landed on an electric eel? (Eels are nocturnal; be a man and get on that board!)

That rational voice was a bastard, but his arguments were irrefutable, so I took a few swift steps up the ladder to the board and launched myself off the end, my body arched, my hands held out in front just as my swimming teacher had taught me many years before, breaking the surface tension with my fingers before the rest of me plunged through. My swimming teacher may have been happy with the dive had she seen it, but unlike me she didn't have testicles; I was less impressed, as they somehow got slapped hard enough that I felt them in my throat. Clearly I should worry less about animals in the lagoon and concentrate more on my own poor form.

Once my testicles had recovered from the dive, I resolved to take full advantage of the lagoon and go for a swim each day. I planned on building slowly until I could swim to the other side and back, around four hundred metres all up. Not so great a challenge, but on my first attempt I wasn't even halfway across when I felt my legs lagging, and my head sinking lower with each stroke. I was doing breaststroke, my bobbing dome unintentionally mimicking the monkeys that watched from the far shore, dipping their heads up and down as they tried to figure out what that strange and inelegant blob was in the lagoon.

Wisely deciding to avoid the embarrassment of needing rescue, I swam back to the swimming platform just as one of the guides, a perpetually upbeat chap called Gustavo, began setting up rods for his guests to go piranha fishing.

'Are you crazy?' one of them shouted at me in an American accent.

'Nah, Australian,' I replied.

To be honest I wasn't sure how wise it was to be in the water at the same time as the bait (chunks of chicken that the wise piranhas were experts at nibbling off the hook without ever touching the metal), and hauled myself out rather nimbly.

The next day, in spite of the ever-present piranhas, I was determined to make it at least halfway across the lagoon before turning back. But just as I launched myself off the board (this time arching my back sharply like a cocked eyebrow to avoid the indignity I'd suffered the day before), I spotted a head bobbing up and down on the other side of the lagoon, not far from the grassy patch. It was the head of an elderly man staying at the lodge, and he had made it to the other side. Being ruled by testosterone is a pain in the arse sometimes: there was now no way I could only go halfway.

I began my slow breaststroke, feeling the fatigue almost immediately as my muscles complained at such abuse two days in a row. Relief followed as they warmed and momentarily stopped their whining; there was even some joy as I got further than the previous day's capitulation point, but then a weary leadenness set in.

The water was surprisingly warm, the tropical sun maintaining it at a bath-like temperature. But only to a point: when tiredness made my limbs droop down to maybe a foot in depth the water suddenly became startlingly cold, jerking me back to proper form. This was a far better way of maintaining style than my old teacher's method of hauling my backside up by the pants anytime I relaxed, giving me a wedgie in the process.

The old man swam past me, heading back towards the lodge, giving a merry '*Ciao!*', my reply a gasped 'Hoo!'—the only sound I could manage at that point.

Somehow I made it to the other side, where I trod water a while, then steeled myself to head back; as I set off the deck looked ridiculously far away, a moon landing of a swim. While I splashed and dog-paddled I distracted myself by listening to the birds around the lagoon's edge, doves cooing, the rasped call of hoatzins interrupted by the odd clapping of wings as they lifted off inelegantly. Kingfishers dipped into the water for prey then beat their catch against branches before swallowing it, and from somewhere unseen came the maniacal, funky-rhythmed call of a wood-rail.

Gustavo ('Call me Gus. Only my mother calls me Gustavo, and only then when I am in trouble') was with new guests when I finally got back. Shooting an amused look at me as I hauled myself out, he said to his group, 'I recommend swimming to you all, you can see it is safe, but maybe don't go across to the other side. Just stay around the platform.' I wondered if there was something I'd missed on my list of potential diving-board disasters. I meant to ask Gus later on why he had said to stay near the platform, but figured it was just because he didn't want to have to canoe out to rescue them should they lose energy.

•

Within days I was doing the swim across the lagoon with relative ease, and was planning on building up to two laps. My only fear was of caimans. Two different species of caiman lived in the lagoon: the inoffensive spectacled caiman (never a problem even when it reached its maximum length of just over two metres), and the black caiman, a confirmed man-eater in some parts of South America, and the largest of its family, reaching six metres in some places.

'There's a large black caiman in there,' Gus told me one day, conversationally.

'Huge?' I asked, echoing Marcello from the Pantanal.

'Not huge. Just large. Maybe three metres. But it usually stays over the other side of the lagoon, near that channel the canoes use to bring guests in.'

'Usually' is not a comforting word when applied to wildlife, as animals are as changeable as the weather. 'Three metres' was even less so, as a caiman that size would be more than capable of dragging me down, pulling me apart, and snacking on me as needed while my bits decomposed. (I think about crocodilians a lot, so I know every grim step of the process.)

He scratched his chin thoughtfully, and added, 'And that caiman under the deck; even though she's just a spectacled she might get upset if she thought you were going for her babies . . .'

'And how big is she?'

'About two metres.'

Two metres wasn't that comforting either. I'd known about the caiman under the deck, but was yet to see it and hadn't realised it was quite so large. Suddenly the diving board seemed the least of my challenges as I tried to gather back the bravery that I'd lost at my desk job.

The same night as my conversation with Gus about the caimans, instead of eating at the main area of the lodge there was a barbecue dinner on the deck. Meat sizzled and delicious aromas drifted through the lodge, making stomachs gurgle hungrily.

I joined a small cluster of tourists and a guide making their way to the deck, following our noses, when a voice from the water called 'Mom!', and I was transported back to Parque Machia in Bolivia, and Sonko the overweight puma.

At Machia, when the volunteers walked towards the pumas' cages they shouted out '*Hola!*' so the puma knew who was walking towards them (since the animals are tied up or caged it would be stressful for them to hear only footsteps). Roy always answered with a hearty, snarling yowl. The plump, strange-voiced Sonko squeaked out something that sounded like a cigarette-smoking, sea-urchin-gargling baby American—'Mom!' he squeaked. 'Mom! Mom!' This sound was also very similar to the plaintive cry of a baby crocodilian.

Now, hearing this sound coming from under the steps leading to the deck, I knew it was not some lost child, but a baby caiman. They can be quite cute, so I stepped off the deck for a closer look, walking down to the water's edge. Rookie error, that move.

'Mom!' came the sound again, but unlike old Sonko, who was just saying hello, this baby caiman meant exactly what it said.

'Bugger,' I thought, just as a wave started coming towards me. I jumped backwards, then sideways, scrambling for the stairs. One of the other tourists staggered away with his hands over his eyes, sure I was about to be eaten, while another gave a strangled croak. Then the guide, who had stepped away for a moment, came back, took in the scene and laughed. He bent down and shone his torch under the deck.

Mom was only about a metre long.

Probably not worth the reaction then.

Based on Gus's exaggeration of the deck caiman's size I decided that the black caiman who apparently lived across the lagoon was most likely not the alleged three metres either, and decided to give it no more thought.

•

With my confidence renewed, the next day's swim was a pleasure, and I started doing one and a half laps. Although I was no longer worried about the caiman, I felt a mild concern about candiru, a fish that makes you understand just how mean a streak evolution possesses. Small and narrow, like half a worm, it usually latches onto the gills of larger fish, lodging itself in with sharpened fins and feeding on the soft flesh inside. Somehow it has also developed a sideline hobby with swimming humans, homing in on the smell of urine before proceeding straight up the urinary tract—this applies to women as well as men. (However, the reputation it has of being able to swim straight up the urinary stream of anyone foolish enough to pee into the river is a myth.) Once inside the urinary tract, the candiru's barbed fins come out and it eats away, driving the host mad with pain—rumours abound of men performing autopeotomies rather than live with it inside them.

I had been told that candiru were not in the lagoon for the same reason there were no mosquitoes—the water was too acidic. Nevertheless, I was glad for the mesh insert in my swimmers that would act as an extra barrier. I also, as a matter of course, did not pee in the lagoon, something that made me swim faster each time my feet dragged into the cold water below.

One day during my swim I noticed a clump of vegetation that must have broken away from the bank or come in on a channel, and had formed a floating island in the lagoon. About two metres in diameter, it drifted randomly, pushed by wind and what small currents there were in the water, until it came to rest right in the middle of my usual route. I would have to pass right by that, and it perturbed me. Such places are havens for fish, who use them to shelter from dive bombers like kingfishers, and trawlers like terns and skimmers.

Unfortunately, it doesn't save them from predators that they share the water with; in fact, any enterprising caiman would investigate the island to see if it was snack time.

These were not good thoughts to be dwelling on as I approached it, and I swam even more slowly than usual, only spurred on when my feet hit the cold patches. For some reason I started to picture myself doing a similar swim in northern Australia, or back in Botswana, and how terrifying it would be if a scaly head appeared beside me. I couldn't help imagining the terrifying feeling of jaws clamping on a limb. I started swimming faster, powering past the makeshift island, the urge to have a little pee stronger than ever before, the fear of candiru still sufficient to keep it in. My swimming technique is all enthusiasm, no style (I'm terrified of hearing that I am the same in bed), and now I was really churning the water, sure that something was stalking me, the mysterious black caiman somewhere behind me, closing in.

I began to plan what I would do if I was grabbed. 'Crocodilians have sensitive skin between their toes,' a guiding instructor once told me in all seriousness, 'and a good pinch there might make them release you.' I couldn't imagine having the presence of mind to locate this particular patch of skin in such circumstances—in fact I thought it was far more likely I'd panic to death first. A friend of mine in South Africa once had a smallish croc take his arm clean off, not something I wished for but better than being grabbed by the torso and dragged down into the water and drowned. If I was fortunate enough to only lose a limb, my board shorts had a drawstring, and I could rip that out and make a tourniquet, swimming to whatever bank was nearest, making sure to compensate for my lopsidedness as I went.

There was a flaw in my plan though. 'Bloody piranhas,' I thought. With that much blood in the water there was no way they would stick with their mainly vegetarian ways.

None of these ideas was comforting in the least, and when I hit my turnaround point I didn't even pause, just started back, taking a wider route around the sinister vegetation.

Suddenly some nostrils appeared beside me, and kept pace. I made a sobbing wail, a panicky flurry from my legs sending ripples over the animal's nose and making it disappear, which was even worse than being able to see it.

My mind took a moment to process what I had seen, busy as it was reverting to childhood; then I realised that the nostrils had been tiny, and closely spaced—a reptile to be sure, but no caiman. The nostrils reappeared, then a whole head—that of a terrapin. ('Tortoises live on land, and have little round feet like elephants,' I have explained to many a tourist. 'Turtles live in the ocean and have flippers. Terrapins live in fresh water and have webbed feet.') 'You bastard!' I spluttered in relief. Once my heart rate had returned to normal, I began to enjoy the little reptile's company alongside me (and I also thought it might act as bait for anything larger that might come along, distracting it from my flailing legs in the water). It tracked with me for a while, and keeping my focus on it rather than the boogey caiman, I was able to enjoy my swim once more, not even flinching too much or squealing when submerged vegetation brushed my leg.

Despite my fears I went back into the lagoon day after day, plunging off the board, swimming out and back, then out and back again, eventually building up to three times across—no great achievement, but after a year on the road it was refreshing to not feel like a piece of cheese.

In Africa I had met and become friends with two well-known wildlife photographers, Pete and Renee, who lived in Ecuador and had introduced me to Sacha's owners, thus facilitating my stay. During my last few days at Sacha they came to visit the camp and get some photos for their portfolios. I pointed out to them a place where the pygmy marmosets crossed a path within the lodge grounds each day, one of them carrying a thumb-sized baby with an old-man face, then announced that I was off for my daily swim.

'How far do you go?' Pete asked.

'Three times across and back,' I answered proudly.

'I wouldn't,' Pete said simply. Pete has lived in Ecuador for twenty-five years, and travels the world photographing animals, getting the very first images of certain species in the wild, so when it comes to wildlife he's someone to listen to.

So I didn't listen and went out to swim the last few days.

Pete and Renee stayed on at the lodge after I left, and emailed me a few days later. 'Remember that story we told you about the Peruvian primate researcher?' they wrote.

I did recall the story. The researcher had disappeared two years earlier while taking his regular swim somewhere in Peru's Manú National Park. No trace had been found, not a scrap of flesh, not a piece of swimwear. If a caiman had grabbed him or if he had somehow been nabbed from the shore by a jaguar there would have been some grisly evidence, and if he had merely drowned it would have become evident over time when his body appeared. There was only one reasonable suspect.

'Well, the day after you left,' the email continued, 'an anaconda was seen coiled right at the place you used to turn around. We couldn't see how long it was because it was piled up, but one section was as thick as a thigh. That could easily take a man.'

'Bugger,' I thought. 'An anaconda. Didn't think of that one.'

A Month of Monkeys

Another of my adventures at Sacha occurred in the jungle.

It was all the monkeys' fault.

And the birds'.

Or maybe mine.

Not only was there a staggering six hundred bird species around Sacha Lodge, there were also eight species of monkey. This amazed me—the whole southern African region holds only two species of monkey, and Sacha is an island of just a few hectares, surrounded by oil interests and illegal forestry and poaching. Yet squirrel monkeys, black-mantled tamarins, rare night monkeys, and the incredibly cute pygmy marmosets could be seen around the lodge, with other, shyer, species staying further out in the jungle.

In the month I spent at Sacha I set myself the challenge of seeing all eight species of monkey. In three weeks, with some effort, I'd seen seven of them. So I was unusually delighted when a fig hit me while I was out on a trail one day and the fruit flinger turned out to be the eighth monkey species, a dusky titi.

Soon after the dusky titi and its family had scampered off I became distracted by a mixed flock of birds moving through the jungle undergrowth. Next thing I knew I was starting to tick off species from my bird list as well. My progress on the trail was slow, but only because I was so enthralled by its bounty. Meanwhile the animals were distracting me from something I should have been paying attention to: the time.

By now I was allowed to walk the trails by myself, far from the madding tourists. I had somehow mastered the art of seeing monkeys, discriminating between branches shaken by a breeze and those that were moving due to the weight of an animal. But the real trick is to see the monkeys without them seeing you. So after the titis had moved on and the birds had dispersed, I was very proud when I saw some howler monkeys coming my way and managed to hide against a tree trunk before they spotted me.

I'd imagined the jungle in Sacha would be a place of impenetrable growth, a thick green barrier filled with snakes and hairy tarantulas, with plenty of cover to make it easy for me to view wildlife. Real rainforest, if left undisturbed, has such a closed canopy that less than ten per cent of sunlight gets through; as a result, not much grows in the understorey at all, and there are few snakes or spiders to be seen. Howlers would normally only be found in primary forest, but even at Sacha that was rare and this family was moving through a relatively open area. It was remarkable that the howler monkeys didn't see me (and pleasing, as I didn't want to disturb their natural behaviour) but they soon settled in a tree above me, getting ready for the night. I stayed motionless for a while, and I was just beginning to wonder if I was jungle-savvy enough to sneak away without disturbing them when the male made a noise like an engine starting.

Soon the whole family (of whom I counted five) joined in the howling, and I was subjected to an ear-rattling cacophony. Looking through binoculars, I focused on the male's throat pouch, which was ballooning with each long breath. The little ones did their best to imitate their dad, their cheeks stretching close to bursting. After a wild lion's roar up close it was the second best thing I'd ever heard, and I was transfixed—so transfixed in fact that I didn't realise that the monkeys were shouting at the dusk, and it was about to get dark. Day length is constant at the equator, and there was no excuse for me to be surprised at sunset occurring at six, just as it did every night.

'Bugger,' I thought, far later than I should have. Despite the relatively light cover compared with rainforest, it was already very dark at tree level. I needed to decide whether to backtrack as quickly as possible along the path I was familiar with or carry on ahead in the direction I was pretty sure would take me to the lodge. Many of the forest trails at Sacha are like orgying anacondas, twisting and crossing each other with no discernible pattern, which made doubling back the sensible thing to do. So I didn't.

Instead, plunging ahead I found that the trail looped away from where I wanted it to go, and became harder to make out. Sadly, my survival skills didn't extend to making a flashlight out of available resources, which at that point were mainly decaying leaves—and mosquitoes. Lots of them. Fallen leaves in the jungle acted as cups for rainwater and made perfect breeding grounds for bloodsuckers. So I ploughed on in the gathering darkness, breathing harder, inhaling a mosquito or six at one point and coughing, enough to make me panic a little. Or maybe the panic was just because I knew I'd been stupid. If it was Africa all I could do at that point was climb a tree and hope I was found by people before a leopard noticed me, but here I knew that I didn't really have cats to worry about, since pumas—though ubiquitous in many parts of South America—had not been recorded at Sacha. (And as Marguerite had pointed out I was more likely to be impregnated by a llama than get lucky and see a jaguar.) The sensible thing to do was sit tight, wait, and see if anyone noticed my absence, though even if they did they'd have no idea where to begin looking for me. Covering myself with my poncho and some insect repellent to slow the loss of blood to the insects, then waiting for morning and backtracking was another sensible option.

So I didn't do that either.

As the darkness deepened I became very aware of the smells of decaying leaves, the screeching of insects, and the low throb of some unknown toad or frog. Then after a while I realised the low throb was actually the sound of the lodge's generator, and began to hope that maybe it wasn't so far away. Unfortunately, just as the canopy swallows light, forest absorbs sound.

By this stage it was so dark in the forest I could barely see, but I was still on some sort of trail, and I tried to follow it. My wonky hearing often has me heading in the wrong direction—but this did not appear to be the case now because the sound of the generator seemed to be getting louder. I didn't know if the trail would continue in the right direction. And if it diverted I wasn't sure whether I should ignore the sensible option (again) and go cross country towards the sound. Stumbling on blindly in the dark relying on my unreliable hearing would be an act of grand tomfoolery, even by my standards.

Then I lost the option of choosing to be an idiot and had it thrust upon me. The villain was a dastardly root which wrapped itself around my boot and tripped me. I swivelled in the air, landing on my back, arched over my pack, instinctively clutching my binoculars high and safe. I scrambled up again quickly, worried about army ants and any other thing that might want to crawl on me and bite, then realised I'd lost any sense of direction I might previously have had. Shaking damp leaves from my hair, I looked around for the trail but couldn't even see my feet. I was now immersed in a darkness so complete it was unlike anything I'd ever experienced.

Cursing myself for not replacing the blown bulb in my Maglite, I slowly and cautiously made my way forward, hands outstretched, breath so ragged it sometimes drowned out the noise I was trying to follow.

Then I saw a light. It was red and pulsed as I moved, as if trying to signal me through the foliage. Convinced it was the lodge, obscured by swaying branches, I slid my feet in its direction, but it was now to my left, so I changed course, and it did too, baffling me momentarily until it winked at me then zoomed up into the air. Red fireflies? I wondered, only familiar with the green ones the rest of the world possesses. The Amazon is a one upper when it comes to insects, which are all brighter, bigger and/or louder than their equivalents in other parts of the world, or just so strange they appear to be the result of some bizarre experiment.

I pushed ahead again, my palms forward, my legs moving in a blind zombie shuffle. After a while, my hands brushed something soft and furry. I flinched back, stumbling again, and bounced off a tree. Suddenly I felt claws clutching me from all sides, and flailed, terrified. Something was biting me, tearing at me.

Despite my fear, I forced myself to stay still and think rationally. The furry thing I'd felt was most likely balsa fluff—drifting cotton from a kapok tree—though in my head I was sure it was a big ugly tarantula, hairy and mobile, like a Russian's knuckles going for a walk. Luckily the claws turned out to be nothing more than thorny vines, which I picked my way out of. Incapable of stopping now, I blundered on, the generator noise definitely louder, the path definitely gone.

'Go to the light!' friends of faith have implored me over the years. And I finally did. Ahead of me a light pulsed; at first I thought it was just another firefly flaunting its freedom, but it came again, not blinking, just strobing in and out of my vision as the angle between it and the foliage changed. I made a beeline towards it, stumbling forward, finally tripping on a raised walkway, then sprawling once more, my hands in front of me balled into fists in case of spiders.

Next thing I knew I smashed into hard timber, falling down. I got up, too thrilled to feel much pain, felt my way to the entrance, and shuffled into the lodge feeling jubilant. I had no idea what time it was, and just hoped a search party hadn't formed.

I short-cutted through the back of the lodge and dashed into my room without passing any staff. It was 7.45 pm. I had been lost for less than two hours, and was only a few minutes late for dinner.

During the meal there was an announcement that Dan would be leading a night walk; thinking it would probably be good to get straight back on the tarantula, so to speak, I arrived before anyone else at the designated meeting place for the walk. A halogen lamp illuminated the spot, and bugs of hallucinogenic diversity dipped and dived at it, some bouncing off, stunned, into the grass below. When a lurid green cicada with bright red eyes did just this, I reached down to grab it and take a closer look. The shadow my arm cast swelled and lengthened, as if a giant were probing the earth, and the shadow of a twig made a dark stripe on the lawn close beside it.

'That twig looks a bit like a snake,' I thought. Just then the 'twig' flicked a forked tongue at my arm. I retracted the limb with such speed it may have made a sonic pop, and Dan arrived soon after to find me sprawled on the deck trying to get a closer look at what he quickly identified as a cat-eyed snake.

'Mostly harmless,' he said. 'Lucky it wasn't a fer-de-lance,' he added, naming one of the region's most venomous and aggressive snakes. If it had been a fer-de-lance (or a viper or bushmaster, two of South America's other venomous snakes), I would have been at serious risk of losing a limb, if not my life.

No matter how well I had hidden from the howlers, clearly I was not in possession of proper jungle skills. There and then I decided that not only was I ill-suited for a return to guiding, but that perhaps the jungle as a whole was not a great place for me to spend much more time. After Sacha, I was going to London to visit Lisa, and after a short stay there planned on coming straight back to South America. Perhaps the sensible thing would be to stay in the UK and give up my wanderings. Maybe I'd been right after all when I left the bush and went back to Australia.

'Nah,' I thought. 'Time to go deeper.' And with that idea began my most extreme journey so far.

Meeting the People

'Man, what happened to your face?' Tom asked me in his usual jovial tone, his Southern accent pronounced even though he'd lived in Ecuador for more than twenty years. Beside him stood a man I knew must be Otobo. Little more than five foot tall but powerfully built, he greeted me warmly. We were in Coca, a small town close to Sacha; from here I would head further into the Amazon basin, where I would visit Otobo's tribe, the Huaorani.

'Muggers,' I explained to Tom, a friend of friends. 'Three of them. And I'd had enough to drink to think it was a good idea to fight back. Probably wasn't,' I finished, indicating my black eye and swollen lip, still prominent two days after the event.

Tom translated this into Spanish for Otobo, no doubt being more than a little generous about my prowess. Otobo nodded at me, apparently impressed at my warrior spirit. Perhaps my misshapen nose (a product of genetics, not fighting) gave the impression that I fought a lot. And lost often.

'All three ran from me,' I carried on, encouraged, but then some fondness for honesty made me add, 'Admittedly by then they had twenty dollars and a credit card.' Tom again translated, but even with my limited Spanish I could tell he was once again speaking up my fighting abilities. It hadn't been much of a brawl—my style was less martial arts and more crazed raccoon—but it had reminded me that not everyone I met on this trip would be friendly.

That we were standing in the somewhat modern streets of Coca having this meeting at all was quite remarkable, as the Huaorani only became aware of the outside world—and the world of them—in the late 1950s. The tribe's name means 'the people', as they consider outsiders of any ethnic group to be something else, usually *cowode*, a term that can be roughly translated as 'cannibal'. Since their introduction to the outside world they have been the targets of missionaries and ruthless oil companies, the two groups sometimes working in cahoots to drive them from their land.

Otobo had met Tom and his wife Mariela when they helped a neighbouring tribe, the Kichwa, set up an ecotourism operation. Even though some of his family had dabbled in working for the oil companies and others had strayed to cities, Otobo saw that perhaps the only way to preserve his culture would be to start his own tourist operation, and let outsiders see how and where the Huaorani live. I was to spend three weeks with him, three weeks of no telephones, internet, newspapers or modern distractions of any kind. With the Minke in London and no way to communicate with her I kept a diary for the first time in twenty years; as it turned out, my time with the Huaorani would be some of the most extraordinary weeks of my life.

•

Three English tourists met Tom, Otobo and myself and we set off from Coca on an open-backed truck with bench seats, driving along the Via Auca (literally 'Road of Savages', a name given by the oil companies who had the road built, and a label the Huaorani are none too keen on). Until its construction, most Huaorani had lived deep in the rainforest, usually far from major waterways, relying on the forest, not water, for their livelihood. These habits had allowed them to stay undetected for so long, but as more roads were proposed their isolation was under threat.

Along the way several other Huaorani people that Otobo knew flagged us down and jumped on board. After several hours on a road well cared for by the oil companies we came to a checkpoint that marked the entry to Yasuni National Park, where military officials checked our health papers and stamped us in, as if we were leaving Ecuador and entering a whole new country. In the minds of the Huaorani, of course, we were. This was their land.

After the checkpoint we transferred to motorised canoe, travelling for several more long hours down the Cononaco River. Otobo was very proud of his vessel, a long river craft made of fibreglass; its modern appearance became increasingly out of place the further we went into the park, seeing fewer and fewer signs of development, then no sign of humanity at all.

We camped in dome tents by the river that night, and Otobo's travelling companions introduced themselves to us, some in Spanish that Tom translated, others in their native language of Huao (which is pronounced as a quite lovely 'Wow'). Everyone's introductions were brief, except for one guy's, who rambled on forever about which village he was born in, where he grew up, and innumerable other details. 'I don't like flies,' he even said at one point. Tom just let him go on, afterwards explaining that he had a reputation for aggression.

Then we four newcomers were given Huaorani names, a process that the five or so of them all meditated and consulted over. Mine was Ayare, because I reminded them of someone of that name, who was tall. (Most Huaorani are barely above five foot, so I *am* tall in their part of the world.) He was also known as a flirt, I was told, good with the ladies, and I'm sure that with my black eye I must have seemed a real catch.

An owl called throughout the night, a mournful and sleep-defying cry. The next day Otobo described it to us as: 'A really big one. Bigger than an eagle. Bigger than a man even.' Later we found the owl in question. It was maybe a foot or so in size, but of course from the ground it did look huge. So therefore to the Huaorani it was.

Setting off in the canoe I soon learnt why the Huaorani traditionally don't wear clothes. It rains here furiously, at least once a day—and I was there in the dry season. In the wet season it rains twice a day. Clothes get soaked and there's no time to dry them before the next drenching, creating a perfect environment for fungi and parasites. It is only in the open spaces directly over the river that any light can penetrate, so after our day's drenching Otobo steered the boat down the middle of the river, swerving only for stumps and the occasional river dolphin. We camped another night, and spent another full day puttering downriver before finally reaching Otobo's village, a three-building affair named Boanamo which is home to Otobo, his wife and their three children, plus any one of his three brothers who might pass through. Only a few hundred metres away was another high-arched thatched building, which housed Otobo's parents, their pet macaw, several dogs and a spider monkey who hissed his bitey intent at any approach. I was introduced to Otobo's father, Omagewe, a diminutive but muscular man in his sixties. He spoke no Spanish, only Huao, so smiled and laughed in greeting.

The English tourists whose trip I had piggybacked in on were keen bird watchers, and that suited me pefectly. I knew from my time in Africa that bird watchers usually spot more animals than anyone else as they are attuned to picking up the smallest movements, the slightest differences in colour, and know how to sit patiently and quietly to see what appears. So it was that we spent our first full day off the canoe at a salt lick, watching rainbow-coloured streams of parrots flutter down to eat the nutrient-rich clay that counters various toxins in their food.

'So, you going to get naked?' Tom asked me. One of the guides at Sacha who had had some dealings with the Huaorani had told me that they would never trust anyone in clothes; only if you're naked can they be sure you're not hiding anything.

'Sure,' I replied. 'But they're all in their seventies,' I indicated the English, 'so I don't imagine they want to see me nude, nor me them.'

'The reason I asked is that Omagewe,' Tom indicated Otobo's father, 'was laughing earlier and saying you should take your pants off.'

'Really? I had no idea we'd become so close already.'

Tom just laughed, and I sat watching the birds and my fellow travellers: Quiet Chris, a softly spoken, well-travelled and pleasant man, who was a friend of the other two, a married couple—Mute Elizabeth, whom I never formed an opinion of because she never spoke, and her husband Stinky Fred, who had plenty of personality, unfortunately not all good. He belonged to a generation who believe it's okay to be racist and misogynistic as long as you wink at the end of each statement to show it's all good fun. And he smelled. We'd been asked not to use the insect repellent DEET, or even deodorant, as it would frighten off animals, but he took this to rule out bathing altogether. It was hard not to retch when downwind of him, but on the plus side he did attract lots of intriguing insects.

For my part I was bathing, in the chocolate milk–coloured waters of the Cononaco River, but cautiously. There *were* candirus here, and caiman, stingrays and hidden stumps. I also had a sizable gash on the back of my head, due to one of my assailants breaking a beer bottle over it during the mugging. Occasional slivers of glass still emerged from the swollen wound that I was treating with nothing but pawpaw ointment. I was vaguely concerned that this might attract piranhas, but not so much that I would take Stinky Fred's route and not bathe at all.

•

December twenty-fifth 2010 was a day of good and bad news. Christmas was never a big deal in my household so means little to me, and even less to the Huaorani, although they did make an effort to honour the strange ritual of the *cowode* by prepping a smoked chicken for us. With no refrigeration it would be the last store-bought meat of our stay, and any other protein would come straight from the jungle.

The day itself involved more birdwatching, some pleasant poking around in the jungle, and a bit of a paddle on the river in a borrowed canoe, Omagewe laughing from the bank at my steering issues (mine was the only canoe tacking like a yacht; for some reason I could not make the bloody thing go straight). Later, Omagewe told us he had found a nest nearby belonging to a harpy eagle, one of the world's most powerful birds and something I was very eager to see. As I was somewhat more nimble than the English I agreed to go ahead and check out the hunting trails leading to the nest. The good news was that it wasn't too strenuous a walk, but the bad news was that it wasn't a harpy eagle, rather an ornate hawk eagle—still impressive and beautiful, but like seeing an ocelot when looking for a jaguar.

That night, though, disaster struck as I made my way into my small tent. A searing pain hit my hand as I undid the zip, and I turned ashen-faced to Otobo's brother Bartolo who was standing nearby.

'Mariela! Tom!' Bartolo shouted. 'Peter's been bitten by a snake!'

The good news was that he was wrong. It was a Konga ant. The bad news was that these are the size of a bullet and pack as much ill intent. Some people bitten by it have fevers that last for days. I took some painkillers, writhed a while, and eventually fell asleep.

No fever eventuated, and the next day was my birthday. This concept is also alien to Huaorani, who have no real idea when they were born; to them it simply does not matter. Any day can be special in the jungle, whether it brings food, a new baby, or a pleasant reunion with family.

That day I saw several new species of bird, and was treated by Mariela and the kind but bemused Huaorani to a birthday cake made from two pancakes on top of each other held together and slathered on top with Nutella. The real treat though was meeting Otobo's father-in-law, a smiling older fellow, around five foot one, with an impressive mullet. Together with Omagewe, he chanted a history to us. It basically listed all the people the men had killed—Otobo's father-in-law had managed five in a 'war' with *petroleros* (oil workers) back in the seventies.

Later that evening I saw a spectacular hummingbird, large for the family at the size of a starling, with tail streamers that curved and crossed each other, covered in iridescent red plumage. Called the fiery topaz, this bird was very high on my wish list, and seeing it made up for some earlier disappointment when Bartolo spotted a tapir ahead of a canoe we were in, but I just missed it, seeing only the bushes rustling as it scampered away. Still, the sighting filled me with a certain optimism. Everything felt like it was getting closer. A jaguar must be nearby. The Huaorani were right—any day could be a special one in the jungle.

The next day we spent four hours in the canoe, travelling downriver to a village called Bameno. In the seventies, this place had been an oil exploration camp, but the Huaorani drove the *petroleros* out (with spears) and took over the property to stop them returning, thus inheriting a gravel airstrip that they have maintained in rough form to this day.

The village, with maybe fifty inhabitants, was far busier than Otobo's little spot upriver (which bears the confusingly similar name of Boanamo), and normally had only five or six inhabitants, swelling to ten if his wife arrived with their three children. (Otobo and his wife have two girls and a newborn son. 'He has six fingers on each hand!' Otobo told me proudly, 'and six toes too!' The toes, I might add, are on his feet where they should be.)

Everyone was related in some way, which might account for the occasional surfeit of fingers and toes, and the Huaorani as an ethnic group only number about two thousand individuals, as they have done for hundreds, even thousands, of years. This meant that if you made one enemy you made many, and as I am constantly making faux pas in my own culture I was quite nervous about offending someone here by accidentally making a gesture that signified: 'Why yes, sir, I would very much like to have congress with your chicken!' Fortunately the villagers of Bameno were nothing but friendly, and curious.

At the airstrip we said farewell to Quiet Chris, Mute Elizabeth and Stinky Fred, and hello to two new arrivals. Then we got naked.

Or at least three of us did, including me. In full Huaorani regalia—that is, nothing but a string, which I plan on wearing until it drops off (at the time of writing it still resolutely circles my waist)—we met the whole village, before making our way to the house of Omagewe's father-in-law Quempere, the jaguar shaman. Among the Huaorani he is considered one of the most powerful spiritual leaders, and is believed to have access to spiritual realms and an ability to change into a jaguar at will. 'I'd love to see that,' I said to Otobo.

'It doesn't happen every day now like it used to,' he explained. 'Why not?'

'He looks after his grandkids a lot now, and they piss on him.'

'Oh,' I said, not really sure what else to say.

Otobo sensed my confusion. 'The jaguar spirit doesn't like the smell, so stays away.'

'Oh,' I said again, and left it at that.

Despite his inability to shape shift, Quempere did give me the heartening news that he would send the spirit of a jaguar to the river's edge, or somewhere in the forest where I would see it.

Then, being me, I dived into the Cononaco River which flows past the village, and swam about a kilometre. There was no real reason why I did it, but public nakedness had fostered a certain delirium, making me forget what I was offering as bait in waters that hold caiman, piranhas and the dreaded candiru.

That night we camped downstream, accompanied by several of the village elders. The new tourists included American Allan, an aspiring television presenter, and his cameraman Fernando, who delighted in the playful nature of the Huaorani men, particularly Otobo's father. I had begun to think of the old man as the Amazing Omagewe. Despite his age he climbed trees as if they were ladders, laughing all the way, while I watched in admiration below, wanting to join in but fearing abrasions on areas that were already sensitive due to being sunburnt for the very first time.

That night we took a cruise in the canoe to look for caiman. I sat in the bow with a hefty Maglite, and eventually I made out a reasonable-sized caiman on a bank (Marcello would have undoubtedly called it 'huge!'). On the way back I continued to shine the torch on the banks, and not far from our camp I hit eyeshine.

'*Tigre!*' shouted Otobo.

When the Spanish arrived in South America they decided that the large spotted cat they encountered was somehow the same as the huge striped one in Asia, so they called it '*tigre*', though of course it wasn't a tiger. So confusingly in South America *tigre* means jaguar. At Otobo's shout I almost fell out of the canoe in excitement, peering with eye-straining intensity down the flashlight's beam.

But this was not a jaguar. It was an ocelot. Roughly twice the size of a housecat with an intricately patterned coat and large eyes suited to nocturnal hunting, it blinked briefly at us then melted into the undergrowth. I felt momentarily deflated, before the optimism I'd learnt in the Pantanal with Marcello came straight back. It was a thrill to see the ocelot as it was the first truly wild cat I'd seen in South America. More would come, surely.

Even Huaorani Fear Someone

I had a fitful night after seeing the ocelot, a fever plaguing my sleep, making me shake under the thin sheet I used as a cover. Tom had suffered dengue fever the year before and said my symptoms were consistent with that disease, something that would require an evacuation, as the Huaorani had no facilities to care for me. I did not want to leave, and in the morning I felt well enough to go out with a group of Huaorani, including the Amazing Omagewe. Probably the happiest man I had ever met, he never stopped laughing or smiling, even when his more aged father-in-law, the jaguar shaman, wandered off into the forest that afternoon after a vision. Tom had explained to me that Quempere was showing signs of senility, so finding him was a priority.

'Quempere! Woo hoo!' Omagewe shouted, then laughed. 'Quempere!'

I joined in with the calling, which for some reason Omagewe found hilarious, all four foot ten of him doubled over with laughter.

'Woo hoo!' we shouted together, and then we both cracked up. It reminded me how much communication can be done without language. Until that day I thought the sound of a champagne cork popping was the happiest sound on earth—now I know it is a group of Huaorani laughing.

We eventually found Quempere back at the canoe, baffled at our concern, using a palm frond as an umbrella against the rain, which was once more lashing down in diagonal streaks, so thick it was blinding. Back at the campsite we gathered at the fire, those of us who were naked standing closer than the others in a communal huddle, laughing at each other's chattering teeth.

That night my fever came back, slow-roasting me for unknown hours until it broke and rivers of sweat soaked my skin. Then, after finally falling asleep (and dribbling into my pillow), I was woken by horrific wailing.

I sat up in shock. My first thought was that our campsite was under attack by the truly wild tribes of Ecuador: the Tagaeri and the Taromenane. The shadow of the two uncontacted tribes loomed over most conversations with Huaorani; they were spoken of with a mix of mythology, curiosity and fear. Everyone had a story about these two tribes that have no contact with the outside world at all; while most of the stories tell of harmless encounters, occasionally meetings can result in great violence. Some years earlier, Huaorani had killed twenty-three Tagaeri in revenge for deaths in their community, even though it turned out the Tagaeri were not responsible. The Huaorani believe that someone is responsible for every death, be it from illness, old age or an attack, and so all deaths must be avenged.

The Tagaeri are close relatives of the Huaorani, but Otobo's family believe the Taromenane are not. As much as the Huaorani seemed completely at one with the forest, they described the Taromenane as being more adept than them in jungle craft, and spoke with a reverence of their abilities. Not long before my visit, Omagewe went hunting for several days, and left his wife alone at their hut in

Boanamo. One night she went outside and saw a group of Taromenane standing at the edge of the field. According to her, they were tall and pale—'as tall and white as you,' she said in Huao, pointing at me. When they spoke she couldn't understand them; she shouted back that they could take what they wanted from the field, then went back inside and waited, hoping not to be speared.

Hearing the screams, my first thought was that surely we were under attack, and in my fevered state my only defence would be to appear so weak I might be spared. The wailing though was short lived, not cut off, and faded to the muttering of someone in a dream state. It had been a nightmare, no more, and while the screamer mumbled themselves back to sleep I lay awake, adrenalin coursing for some time, wondering how close the nearest Tagaeri or Taromenane might be.

Normally I would be excited by the level of mystery surrounding these peoples, but in the pitch black of a jungle night it was just intimidating and I was glad to have the many spears of my new Huaorani friends close by.

•

As a rule I don't believe that any race has more smart or dumb people than any other, or good or bad, and it irritates me when people say things like, 'Oh, you must just love the people in Africa!' as I think it is a sign of covert racism. But among the Huaorani I met more extraordinary people than in any other small group I had ever encountered.

Otobo was a natural host and guide. He effortlessly switched between the demands of the elderly English bird watchers and the more culturally interested Americans, reading their needs as neatly as if he had been to the finest tourism management school. His father was a god in the forest, a hunter of note, capable of turning invisible when he wanted to. Omagewe might also be the most dangerous man I have ever met, with a significant body count of *petroleros* and illegal loggers to his name, yet his good humour and constant laughter made it almost impossible for me to imagine him as a spear-wielding killer.

Then there was Penti, who I met in Bameno. Unlike most Huaorani, who are a stocky people, Penti was slender, and sported a natty Clark Gable moustache. But it was what he said that made him stand out. For more than twenty years he had fought to protect his home from oil companies, and he was articulate and knowledgeable about the challenges the Huaorani face from those who would take their land. Recently, illegal oil exploration had taken place; Penti told me that if he couldn't stop this through legal means it would be solved the Huaorani way, with a spear. He explained that twice before oil companies had been allowed to extract oil from within the national park, and both times it was disastrous. Texaco spilled more oil in the Ecuadorian Amazon than the *Exxon Valdez* did in Alaska in 1989, and the roads that were built through the forest to facilitate the extraction are like leukaemia, spreading the poison of illegal logging and poaching, along with the colonists who move illegally in from outside areas and whom the government has no will to move. These invaders continue to make their way deeper into the park, sullying once pristine blocks of wilderness and encroaching ever more into Huaorani territory.

Many of the Huaorani came to visit our campsite, downstream from Bameno, in canoes, and we travelled back to visit them in Bameno, a torturous journey for me as my fever returned with a vengeance. The sunlight off the water was like spears in my eyes, the roar of the motor deafening. When we arrived in Bameno, Tom, Mariela, Allan and Fernando would fly out, and with some trepidation, but mainly enthusiasm for adventures ahead, I would be left alone with the Huaorani for two weeks.

'Did I scream out last night?' Fernando asked on the canoe. 'I think I was having a nightmare.'

That explained the scream that had woken me the night before. I wasn't surprised Fernando had experienced a nightmare: the very air in this place felt hallucinogenic, or maybe it was just my fever. As soon as we made it to Bameno I curled up to rest in a hammock in Otobo's Bameno home. The house was made of palm poles and thatched with leaves, which offered some respite from the blinding heat outside.

I was woken some time later by a squawking macaw that wandered in, screeched at me several times, then ambled back out. Through gaps in the rough walls I could see village life as it puttered all around, some people cooking, some snoozing, and a desultory soccer game being played so lazily I almost felt well enough to join in. People in various states of undress walked in and out, some shaking me awake to ask questions like: 'In the United States how many wives do you have?' (It didn't matter how many times I said I was Australian, all foreign *cowodes* are from America.)

'I have only one,' I said (they also make no distinction between a wife and girlfriend), 'but she is in England.'

'Huh,' they scoffed, 'you should get more,' then they walked away, chasing out the chickens that came and went as freely as the people.

Otobo told me he needed more than just his current sole wife, but was too busy with his ecotourism business at the moment. The two travelling bands of the last week were the first foreigners many of the Huaorani had seen in more than a year. 'Yes, but I am the busiest tourism operator here!' Otobo said proudly. 'I have many more tourists than anyone else!'

•

As I sat down to write in my diary on the second-last day of 2010, I realised that and I had no idea what day of the week it was, nor any interest in finding out. Dates were becoming as irrelevant to me as they are to the Huaorani. Huao numbers only go as high as twenty; after that they simply use the words for 'a lot' (*nange*) and 'many' (*baco*). Even the numbers they do have are complicated to say—their count goes 'one', 'two', 'two and one', 'two and two', 'five', 'five and one', and so on. Technically you could go higher than twenty, so for example to give my age—thirty-six—I would say: '*Bototepenpoga go tepenpoga go tepenpoga go emempoke go arokai.*' Or I could simply say '*Baco.*'

This complexity is probably why most Huaorani will tell you some patently absurd figure when you ask how old they are. When I asked Quempere's age I was told, variously, 'More than one hundred', 'Somewhere near sixty', and one youngster gravely told me that he was 'probably more than twenty', clearly impressed at such longevity. ('He's probably in his eighties,' Tom had said, 'just based on the age of his children and their children.')

The tribespeople jabbed at my notebook now as I wrote; only the youngest among them and the educated Penti were able to read (and even then they learnt Spanish, not English), but they were all fascinated by the marks I made on the page. It would have felt like a breach of privacy anywhere else, but here it was not at all unpleasant or invasive.

As I wrote that morning the same macaw had walked into Otobo's house again, spoken a few words, laughed, and walked out.

'Great,' I thought, 'even a bloody parrot speaks more Huao than me.'

One of the few terms I had become proficient with was '*waponi*', a versatile word that means 'hello', 'thanks' and 'good'; when said with a smile it covered much of what needed to be said.

Earlier that morning I'd been woken up by the sound of voices. Looking out of my hammock I could see a gap in the wall; peering through this, straight at me, was the jaguar shaman.

'*Waponi*, Quempere,' I said, then added, '*Ibanoimi?*' which means 'How are you?' In reply he laughed, walked in and sat beside me, his wife following. With clawed hands he picked up and studied my hair, teeth and palms, before clapping my hands together, laughing heartily once more.

As he chatted to me in soft tones, his wife (a sprightly sixty or so to Quempere's estimated eighty) laughed at everything he said. The only person I'd felt sorry for in my time there was the aggressive man who on my very first night had spoken at us about his life, including his time with the missionaries, and all he had learnt from them. Throughout his diatribe he'd had his hands clasped in supplication, with the lightless eyes and forced grin of someone who has been told to be happy. Maybe it wasn't the fault of the missionaries, but something was lost in him; he seemed to lack a brightness, a beauty, that the other Huaorani carried so casually.

That afternoon we made our way back upriver to Otobo's place by canoe. After a short break we travelled another hour along the river to an even smaller village than Otobo's. This was the home of a friend Otobo employed to cook for tourists when they came through, who perhaps due to his muscular physique had chosen to go by the Western name of Conan. Many Huaorani used a Western name when dealing with outsiders, perhaps because they couldn't bear the mangling of their native names. In Conan's village, I was surprised to meet the man with the clasped hands from our first night, and to learn he was Conan's brother. He went by the name of Joseph, and was, to his credit, very generous and while he and I practised throwing spears at a banana tree his wife cooked us manioc and fish, served on a palm leaf and eaten with the fingers. We all rinsed our hands in the same tea-coloured water first, and my already queasy stomach initially rebelled. I ate it all though, with a smile as credible as our host's, and had not a single ill effect afterwards.

I began to change my judgement of the man, as his spear-throwing lesson had been a patient and gentle one, despite my obvious ineptitude. He had also pointed out to me some monk sakis in nearby trees, a beautiful woolly-coated species of monkey I'd only seen once before. Joseph was Huaorani, just different, more exposed to the outside world but retaining a generosity common to them all. Maybe this is what all Huaorani would become as the world closed in, maybe not.

Don't Let Me Die This Way

The never-to-be defined illness was just part of a catalogue of misadventures I experienced during my time with the Huaorani, but I was still enjoying every day—apart from a moment on the evening after visiting Conan's village when I almost died.

Earlier that day we stopped at Otobo's place in Boanamo. I helped unload the boat, hauling seats, tanks of water and gas cylinders up a muddy slope. Suddenly everything wavered and I briefly fainted, something I had never done before. Just as Roy had tried to hide his weakness from me, I didn't want the Huaorani to see I was still unwell, so popped back up. The Huaorani laughed, not out of malice, but because it was clearly not anything worth worrying about. And because no matter your culture, a man falling face first into mud is funny. So I burst out in guffaws too, until it made me feel woozy again and I staggered on, followed by chuckles.

An hour later I went to bathe in the river, barefoot and wearing nothing but a swimming costume (this was more clothes than I was normally wearing, but I felt it was an important precaution against candiru). Most of the embankments by the river were muddy and any foot traffic quickly turned the ground into the consistency of chocolate mousse. The trail I walked through led to Otobo's 'beach', a sandy patch that only turned muddy once you were ankle deep, meaning that with some tricky foot shaking you could emerge clean.

On the trail a column of ants, maybe twenty wide, swarmed laterally across my path in a hypnotic stripe of constant movement. I hopped over them, identifying them as army ants. These ants are so feared that even a jaguar will walk around them. Army ants don't look much different to a common garden ant, apart from being slightly larger. Their main difference is the sheer numbers they gather in to launch their marauding attacks, and the columns they travel in. When they fan out in a swarm to forage they devour everything that does not move out of their way, and there are stories of chickens trapped in coops that the ants stripped to the bone in minutes.

The trail of ants doubled back, and crossed the path at another point. I hopped over it again, but soon after the column turned and began to march down the centre of the trail. I waddled along straddling it until it split into two columns, then split again, and I found myself surrounded by multiple lines of ants. Glancing back I saw that the way I had come was now covered, and with no time to think I launched into a run, my tender feet seeking the places with the fewest ants. But the first bites came immediately, causing excruciating pain in both feet, and I broke into a sprint, no longer caring what I trod on.

I would probably have been better off turning back and trying my luck that way. After sprinting for a few steps the world lurched and I felt another faint coming on. I had no time to process the thought, but I instinctively knew that falling here and blacking out would leave me so covered in bites they could be fatal. 'Don't let me die this way,' I thought briefly, recalling stories of elderly people killed because they couldn't move fast enough. A few more bites and the pain they brought, plus a shot of adrenalin, kept me upright until I was finally past the rapidly expanding swarm, and I threw myself down, my feet aflame as I swatted at the ants digging their mandibles into my flesh.

Standing again, I staggered to the water and flopped in, only to find that the bites had paralysed my feet to a degree but hadn't deadened the pain receptors, so agony flared anew. Looking back at the river bank, I could see every grasshopper, mantis and other insect capable of flight taking off in waves as they escaped the voracious army. Soon the beach was covered in black bodies. It was only around a fifty-metre swim to another exit point, but my feet were numb and useless for propulsion, the river was filled with snags, and I knew I was prone to fainting. Swimming back was lunatic. Yet I took one more look at the beach and began careful strokes into the current.

Buggered if I was walking back.

•

After what must have been my first booze-free New Year's Eve in two decades (I was in bed pretty much as soon as it was dark), I spent another feverish night but woke feeling the best I had in some time. So I took a beautiful wooden canoe that was sitting at the village edge filled with water and mud, bailed it out and spent several idyllic hours paddling up the small river that flanks one side of Boanamo before it joins the murky Cononaco.

As I paddled I saw my first ever Jesus lizard, a creature straight out of a cartoon—when startled on the river banks that are its home it rears up on its back legs and whirrs them so fast that it literally walks on water until it reaches safety on the other side of the river. I spent the rest of the day with Omagewe and his wife, who decided to make me some armbands out of palm cotton and strands of Omagewe's hair that he had crudely hacked off with a knife. To make the armbands she quickly built a loom from kindling-sized branches and the tough aerial roots that the Huaorani use for twine, then threaded the cotton and hair round and through these to make a tight weave. These armbands could be worn for dancing, or just because someone felt like having them on. Omagewe sometimes sported a headband when he set out hunting; apparently it signified a message along the lines of 'I come in peace,' should he encounter Tagaeri or Taromenane. This was as elaborate as any clothing went for the Huaorani, and led me to musing about their adoption of Western attire and how they wore it.

A Huaorani fashion parade would be a curious affair. It is only the elderly who regularly dress (or undress, I should say) traditionally, but even Quempere wears a necklace made of red and blue plastic beads interspersed with beads that have random letters of the alphabet he cannot read printed on them. Omagewe walks around in shorts most days, but at home or out hunting he goes naked save the string. One day though he strolled over to me wearing saggy grey underpants so large he had to tuck them into his string, and an oversized fluorescent green T-shirt with 'Abercrombie and Fitch' in grand lettering down the side, a fine counterpoint to the Dolce & Gabana T-shirt Bartolo had sported the day before. They are of course cheap Chinese knock-offs and often have misspellings, or whole words missing, so I was really hoping at some stage to come across someone with an FCUK shirt.

The men also sport some fine hairdos. Otobo's father-in-law, as I've mentioned, could have stepped straight off the cover of a Bon Jovi album (if Jon Bon Jovi were five foot tall, that is). Quempere maintains a traditional style, long, with a dead-straight fringe stopping just above his eyebrows, kept in shape by regular trims with sharpened mollusc shells. Like his father-in-law, Otobo has a fine mullet, and I saw a child in Bameno with a perfect Elvis coif.

As his wife worked, Omagewe kept me entertained with a pantomime of the morning's hunt, during which he'd speared a peccary (a pig-like animal that travels in large herds, clacking their sharp tusks as a warning to any potential predator): all the while he chatted in Huao and laughed, chortling hardest at the part where he fell from a tree and the peccary slashed his ankle with its tusk. Part of the Huaorani's happiness seems to stem from their ability to find comedy in everything. If I saw someone fall out of a tree my Western instinct would be to ask how they were or offer assistance. The Huaorani laugh at them until the person laughs back. Maybe they would respond differently if the situation was life-threatening, but I never witnessed such a situation.

When I returned to Boanamo, Otobo explained to me that the following day I was going to be sent off deeper into the jungle again and would spend the night near one of the salt licks; this might be my best chance of seeing a jaguar at last. Time has almost no meaning in the Amazon, so while my makeshift diary allowed me to keep track of the date I had no idea what hour or day it was, but I did know that the date of my departure from the jungle and the continent was stalking, getting closer, and about to clamp down.

On my London trip to see Lisa I had met up with several of my old safari friends who had been attending a travel trade show, and I had been offered a very intriguing job by one of them. It involved travel—lots of it—and the chance to do good. The company I'd be working for is quite fraudulent, in that it's not really a business at all but a conservation organisation disguised as one. It runs safari camps but uses its profits to protect habitat for animals, sponsor research, and involves communities in conservation projects so they embrace them. I'd decided to take the job, and once I left the Huaorani I would be heading out of South America after almost eighteen months there. I wanted the most from the last few days. Above all, I wanted to see a jaguar.

•

The next morning I didn't go to the salt lick as planned—to the Huaorani, plans are as flexible as time and numbers; while I had found this mildly frustrating at first, I soon found it quite liberating. Instead Omagewe took me for a jungle walk. There is a rhythm to jungle walking. It is less frantic than a city walker's pace, less harried, but it somehow feels faster, more elegant, a glide compared with a thump. A jungle walker's feet must be in tune with their eyes, the same eyes that watch the canopy, the trees, for prey or danger while picking out the quietest and most efficient way of placing each limb. This requires the most intense concentration but is somehow relaxing, like a mobile meditation. Both exhilarating and soothing, it may be our species' oldest and finest art.

I'm crap at it.

Twigs snapped under my feet, branches rustled as my arms brushed against them, and the permanent toothy display of joy I couldn't hide would have been as subtle as Gotham City's bat signal. 'Look! Over there! Hop in the monkey-mobile! It's an idiot!' I could imagine my quarry saying.

Making things worse, I was wearing boots, no doubt a fetching complement to my string, but necessary as my baby-soft feet had me hopping, cursing and stumbling in blind pain whenever I tried walking without them—surely a spearable offence should I chase food away.

For Omagewe the jungle was a book he had read so often that every page was familiar. In Africa I might have advanced to Dr Seuss levels of proficiency; here I didn't even know the alphabet. But as always, Omagewe read his book as a comedy, and regaled me with long incomprehensible tales in Huao peppered with some Spanish words he had just learnt, chuckling as he acted out previous hunts, mainly of peccaries (though for all I knew he might have slipped in a tale or two about picking off oil workers as well).

People I knew who had visited the Huaorani had told me about witnessing the moment when they get 'in the zone', becoming pure hunters. This happened while I was out with Omagewe. He carried just a spear, no blow gun with poison darts, so he could only hunt ground game, but while he was pointing out some woolly monkeys to me they reacted as if he were fully equipped to put a dart in them and took off through the canopy in fright. If he had been hunting and had managed to hit one with a poison-tipped palm arrow he would have had to chase it, as the monkeys don't die immediately. So when these monkeys swung away he shot off along the ground below them, perhaps out of habit, perhaps just for the fun of it; all of a sudden his four-foot-ten frame was an immense advantage. On a level track I am confident of my speed, but here he was swift, silent and agile. I lumbered behind him in my flippety-flappety rubber boots, feeling like a half paralysed elephant seal.

At one stage, while he was still in sight, I saw ahead of him a fallen tree about a foot off the ground; another tree had been brought down and lay parallel above it, leaving a gap of maybe two feet, with lianas framing it on either side. Without breaking stride or losing sight of the monkeys, Omagewe ran straight ahead, jumping at the gap, tucking his legs under and his head down, a mighty ball of muscle with a spear protruding, before starbursting on the other side of the gap and hitting the ground without missing a step. Following him, I ran up to the obstacle, briefly paused, and then made the uncharacteristically sensible decision to run around it. By then, however, Omagewe was out of sight.

Some minutes later he came back, grinning sheepishly, spear still in hand, telling me with gestures and Huao what had just happened, even though I had witnessed most of it. Then he told me again, this time with some monkey noises thrown in. He smiled at me, seeming to want a response.

'*Waponi*,' I said and, as expected, he laughed as if it was the best thing he'd ever heard.

Alone in the Amazon

I was completely alone. In the Amazon. Well, alone as far as human company went. At least eight species of parrot, including three types of macaw, were squawking, cackling, chirping and croaking around me, and I'd been visited by howler monkeys, spider monkeys, and a very large herd of white-lipped peccaries. Due to the peccaries' reputation for aggression I thought it best to entertain them from a perch a little way up a tree, and spent more than an hour there, during which I realised that I had spent more time in trees as an adult than I ever had as a boy, and reflected that this was probably a fine thing.

I had arrived at the salt lick a couple of days later than planned and would stay there for two nights and three days. I had asked to go alone so I could get a real feel for the jungle; I also wanted to give Otobo's family a break from me. With me, I had a small tent, plenty of water, my binoculars, some chocolate that Otobo had miraculously produced, two torches, a spear on loan from Omagewe, and an imagination that just wouldn't stop taunting me with everything that could go wrong. It was exciting, but also very frightening, so to soothe myself I started a list of things that could kill me while I was staying alone at the salt lick, reproduced here:

1. Eyelash viper/fer-de-lance/bushmaster: These three snakes had all been seen in the area. The eyelash viper is known to be

moody—perhaps because it has no hair, let alone lashes (in spite of its name). Those are horns above its eyes—*because it is the devil*. I'd never seen one, but that didn't mean there wasn't one in my tent. The fer-de-lance, meanwhile, has a cross on the back of its head, like a pirate flag without the skull; I presume evolution is working on correcting that omission. And even Roy was afraid of bushmasters: once he saw one outside his cage and refused to come out for the rest of the day. They are pure evil with scales.

2. Jaguar: Now that would be deliciously ironic, wouldn't it?

3. Puma: Yes, getting bitten by a puma a week before leaving South America would bookend my trip quite neatly, but I've never liked bookends.

4. Tagaeri: The number of animals and large birds has increased dramatically in this area since Otobo's clan decided not to hunt here (a decision made in the hope of attracting more tourists). Their abundance might attract the Huaorani's cousins the Tagaeri, though hopefully not in the next two days. Nobody could tell me the likelihood of seeing Tagaeri, as when discussing the tribe's numbers even expert anthropologists become Huaorani and grab a figure from the air. 'One hundred! No, three hundred! One thousand!' Who knew? But I had my spear just in case. Oh goody.

5. Taromenane: This most mysterious of uncontacted tribes might not even exist, according to some anthropologists (who may be funded by the oil companies seeking to justify their exploration of the area). But their purported nonexistence was no good to me if they didn't know about it.

6. Peccaries: Being killed by a peccary would be the most dignity-stripping of the above options, but was still quite possible. If they caught me off guard and felt the need to avenge the deaths of

their brethren at Omagewe's spear tip, I could be slashed and gored to death. Luckily they smell like a wrestler's armpit so I should be able to detect them coming.

And with those pleasant thoughts, I lay down a while. That night I resolved to keep a watchful if bleary eye open for a jaguar, and whatever else might come to my home sweet temporary home.

As darkness fell, I initially found my isolation unnerving. I imagined footsteps (which were probably just leaves falling from trees) and heard breathing (it was my own), so at one point I got up to face it all, grabbed the torch and went for a brief night walk before my nerve failed and I returned to the tent. I didn't see anything noteworthy, and this reassured me enough to drop into a refreshing sleep, from which I awoke every few hours. Each time I woke I shone my torch outside to check for jaguars, or Taromenane, but none appeared. There was always the next night though.

•

On the afternoon of the next day I'd been sitting, concealed, for some time (hours? I had no way of knowing) as parrot species, ranging from enormous macaws to tiny leaf-green parrotlets, all gathered, inching their way closer to the lick, building the nerve to flutter in and get the nutrients they needed from the clay. They were wary of predators, who knew this was a daily ritual; any branch could hide a viper, every shadow some lethal cat.

The parrots were very close to the lick when they erupted into a cacophony of squawks and a shower of fear-induced defecation, the sky filling with colour as hundreds of birds wheeled away. Seconds later a hawk arrowed through with something clutched in its talons—something green, red, and redder still where the twitching body had been pierced.

I never like to see any animals die but I have learnt not to flinch from the reality of nature. In cities we react with abhorrence to any sort of violence, as if blood and death were unnatural, but the animal kingdom shows us otherwise. Maybe that was why I had started laughing during the mugging, a revolutionary moment after too many sanitised experiences. 'Here it is!' I thought. 'This is the real stuff! This is life!' While I'm no fan of conflict, a complete absence of it can also dull humans to the pain of others, as suffering seems only to be on television, and as real as anything else you see there. I'd felt this myself in Sydney, where I had found myself complaining about the most petty of inconveniences as if they were genuine setbacks. On my return to Sydney in 2002, people often asked me what it was like coming back to 'the real world' after so long in the bush. But this was the real world, and a lack of exposure to the blood and guts of living felt like hiding from reality.

Despite all the talk of spearing, the Huaorani aren't violent people. They only kill when the situation demands it. Noting that Huaorani men are built like wrestlers, I had asked Otobo one day about their approach to fighting. He shook his head adamantly. 'No. Huaorani don't like to fight at all! If there is a real problem with someone we just spear them . . .'

•

As my second day at the salt lick drew to a close, I checked that my testicles were still present (they were), urged them to contribute some bravery, and dashed along a path as far as I could before darkness hit, so that I was forced to walk a long way back. Again I saw nothing worth reporting, and yet it remains one of the most frightening things I have ever done. I realised how often I put on a brave face when with others, sometimes *for* them, so my company wouldn't feel scared. Yet, alone on that walk, I had regressed to the boy scared to take the garbage out at night because who knew what monsters lurked along the garden path?

My last night alone in the jungle was also most likely my last good chance to see a jaguar. It was still possible that one would cross my path in the two days I would spend back with the Huaorani before Otobo took me back to Coca, but most jaguars would be too canny for such an encounter. (The last jaguar seen near the villages was six months before my visit; Omagewe speared it because it was eating his chickens.) All this ran through my mind as Otobo came to fetch me in his canoe, and take me back to Boanamo.

•

Perspective is such a fickle thing. I was back at Otobo's village, which felt city-sized and bustling after three days alone. On my first day back at Otobo's village his wife prepared an enormous meal which included paca (a rodent slightly larger than a rabbit). Out here food is valued, treasured even, but there is no refrigeration so when something is abundantly available the people gorge. To begin with I had been eating Western food that had been brought in from Coca, but when this ran out I began eating mostly traditional food with the Huaorani. This included paca and a type of caterpillar; eventually the peccary that had gored Omagewe turned up on my plate.

While I ate the welcome-home feast I watched Otobo's older daughter playing with what I thought at first was some sort of ragdoll, before I realised it was the baby of the paca we were eating for dinner.

Although the small rodent was quite dead, the little girl cooed over it, even wrapping it in a blanket at one point. Later, after one of the dogs had stolen it, she treated a bottle of cooking oil the same way, showing certain instincts are global.

Once dinner was over, the clan piled into a canoe for the short paddle to Omagewe's hut, leaving me alone again. This was their life as they would live it whether I was there or not: some chores, some family time, lots of laughter.

Everyone I have spoken to about the Huaorani believes they will be dragged into our modern world one way or another, and soon; there are any number of groups that want to adopt and help them through the process. But if you asked any parent what they want for their child the first thing they would say is 'happiness'. I have no idea what anyone can teach the Huaorani about that.

While I am perhaps naive in my view of the Huaorani to me their life has the blissful simplicity of those first few months in a relationship when your connection feels pure and perfect and even spinach between your lover's teeth is somehow cute. Surrounded by the abundance of the forest, right now they desire no more because they don't know what else there is to want. Billions of us have moved past that honeymoon stage: we now want too much, and probably can't go back. For us, perhaps—just like in a relationship when the first flush has faded—what's left is to identify what you do love in the world and endure the rest. Maybe what we—what I—needed to do was find what inspires me and fills me with joy, and use the rest of my time on this planet to do something that matters to me.

But as I watched the Huaorani, I knew that I would give all of my clothes, the few other things I owned, even all that I knew of the world, everything but Lisa, to be as shamelessly happy as Omagewe.

The Way Out

The trip out would involve a two-day stint in the canoe, but first Otobo needed to take his youngest daughter back to Bameno, four hours downstream and five back. Always keen to see what wildlife might be beside the river, I piled in too. Big mistake. Unlike the shaded smaller tributaries that criss-crossed around us, the Cononaco was broad, and open. A few days earlier, my camera battery had died, and my sunscreen ran out soon after. The first loss was merely sad, but the second was dangerous considering my new penchant for bare-arsed exploration; very soon not an inch of me was spared from being burnt, much to the Huoarani's amusement. Learning as I was, I had just pointed at my pink bits and laughed back. But while earlier I had been merely pinked, by the end of the day I was traffic-stopping red, and exuding so much heat that Otobo's wife hung wet clothes near me, saying I would dry them faster than the fire. It would have been merely uncomfortable and led to no more than a restless night in my hammock, but I would have to spend two more days in the canoe before hitting Coca and the chance of some soothing lotion, no doubt needed after another two days of skin-ravaging travel to get out.

I waved goodbye to Omagewe and his wife, who would not accompany us, and I wanted to say that my time with them had been fantastic, and to thank them profusely, but was still limited to a mere

'*Waponi*,' which for the first time felt woefully inadequate. Omagewe waved from the bank, laughed, shouted '*Waponi!*' back at me and walked away before we were out of sight, off to live the life he has lived since before outsiders even knew of his existence.

It rained, hard and ceaselessly, for our first day's travel. Even the stoic Otobo took a T-shirt I offered him; although it immediately became soaked it offered some insulation.

My three weeks with the Huaorani had left me bearded, bedraggled and bemoulded, but as we camped in the jungle that night I knew I would miss it painfully. A smoky jungle frog called nearby, one of my favourite sounds. I kept an ear peeled, listening for another sound, one Marcello had taught me—a long rasp of a call that would tell me that there was a jaguar close by—but all that night I lay sleepless, and no such sound came. I wanted the miracle—golden eyes peering from the forest as we broke camp or piled into the canoe, or a flash of fur as we motored along—but this was no fairytale, no fantasy, and a jaguar did not appear.

The next day, we motored upriver for what seemed an anti-climactically short time and arrived back at the checkpoint, and soon after that I was on a bus back to Coca, travelling alongside jungle that had been scorched and slashed.

If I had learnt anything from the Huaorani it was that the trick of life is not to be content with what you have, but to be happy with what you do not. The trip was never really about jaguars anyway, or birds, or about finding myself, losing myself, or defying my age, but about seeking something wild and rare, not just in the jungle, but in me. I'd feared that too many years of desk-bound normalcy had killed off this part of me, but chasing the jaguar took me to so many places that I would never have been if I'd owned a fridge. I came to South

America to find a jaguar, but came away with so much more. I found a truly wonderful girlfriend, a country that made adversity into something uplifting, the scariest pet you could ever have; at the same time, I learnt that constant travel is exhausting, and that maybe, just maybe, it is okay to settle down. For a little while, anyway.

Of course, I didn't find the jaguar, but that just means I have to keep looking.

Afterword

I often wish life was like a story that you could go back and edit if it didn't work out, but I can't think of much that I would change about my eighteen months in South America. Overwhelmingly my memories are happy ones, but some are tinged with sadness.

Hollywood would have us believe that accidents happen in slow motion, and that the greatest challenge to romance is some obstacle and, with that overcome, all will be triumphant. But of course accidents come at full and out-of-control speed like a crazed puma or a raft being sucked into a whirlpool, and the hardest romantic endeavour is not to get together, but stay together. After leaving South America I flew to London to be reunited with Lisa, but I couldn't stay in London long, and the strain of too much time and distance meant that the Minke and I decided to end our relationship. We remain friends, and I will forever be glad for her company through so much of the trip.

At the time of writing I am employed in a job I love, working with colleagues I consider friends and on occasion even respect, travelling the world and quite enjoying the looks people give me when they see the dirty, frayed piece of string around my waist.

Acknowledgements

My sincere thanks go to the following people:

Harris and Marguerite Gomez for giving me the softest landing imaginable in South America, and being such wonderful friends.

Pete Oxford and Renee Bish, wildlife photographers extraordinaire, for saving my bacon, then putting it in some of the most exciting situations I have experienced. Much of this book would not have come about without their advice and introductions.

The Minke, for more than can be said or written.

Tom Quesenberry (now that's a funny name, isn't it?) and Mariela Tenorio, who run the beautiful El Monte Lodge in Mindo, for arranging and assisting with so much of the Huaorani trip, and laughing as heartily as the Huaorani at all my maladies.

Bec Smart, Bondy, Mick Payne, Adrian, Rob Thoren and Nina at Inti Wara Yassi.

Sam Sudar for getting in a car with me.

Julio, the night watchman at Hostel Americana in El Calafate.

Marcello Yndio, for the way he killed a chicken.

Peter Fitzsimmons, for coffee, advice, and constant reminders that he sells more books than me.

Guillerme and Andres at the Sacha office, Tomas the manager, as well as all the staff at Sacha Lodge for making my stay there so pleasurable and monkey-filled.

Aaron Sorkin for answering so many questions, and the Undeletables for laughs and thought-provoking debate.

Marcella Liljesthrom for the swallows.

Friederike 'Wildchild' Wildberg for some wise words, but mainly for being German yet funny.

Lloyd Temple Camp, because he wants to be mentioned in a book.

Donald Brown for the same reason (and yes, yes, yes, it is true, he also kept me employed for several years when few people would).

Tarli Young for saving me from a planned life of luxury and comfort in Costa Rica, and inadvertently sending me to Bolivia and Inti Wara Yassi instead.

Ben and Kate Loxton for insisting I waste some time in debauchery and laugh myself silly while doing so. And Yahtzee too.

Diana Balcazar for expert guiding while filming in Colombia.

Matt Mitchell and Jonny Hall at Hostel Revolution, Quito.

John Purcell and Tamsin Steel for putting me up—and putting up with me—when I was recently single and a moping dullard.

And Louis, Hoens and Jan Louis Nortje who gave me somewhere to stay during the main editing phase of this book, far from South America in Namibia.